THE WIN-WIN SOLUTION

THE
WIN-WIN
SOLUTION

Guaranteeing Fair Shares to Everybody

Steven J. Brams   **Alan D. Taylor**

W. W. NORTON & COMPANY

New York   London

For information about permission to reproduce selections from this book,
write to Permissions, W. W. Norton & Company, Inc.,
500 Fifth Avenue, New York, NY 10110.

The text of this book is composed in Garamond
with the display set in Eras
Desktop composition by Seiji Ogata
Manufacturing by the Haddon Craftsmen, Inc.
Book design by Charlotte Staub

Library of Congress Cataloging-in-Publication Data
Brams, Steven J.
The win-win solution : guaranteeing fair shares to everybody /
Steven J. Brams, Alan D. Taylor.
p. cm.
Includes bibliographical references and index.
ISBN 0-393-04729-6
1. Conflict management. 2. Negotiation. 3. Fairness.
I. Taylor, Alan D., 1947– . II. Title.
MN136.B7318 1999
303.6'9—dc21   98-56036
CIP

W. W. Norton & Company, Inc., 500 Fifth Avenue, New York, N.Y. 10110
www.wwnorton.com

W. W. Norton & Company Ltd., 10 Coptic Street, London WC1A 1PU

1 2 3 4 5 6 7 8 9 0

Perhaps the first moral judgment uttered by the child is,
"That's not fair!"

James Q. Wilson (1993)

RALPH: When she put two potatoes on the table,
the big one and the small one, you immediately
took the big one without asking me what I
wanted.

NORTON: What would you have done?

RALPH: I would have taken the small one, of course.

NORTON: You would? (in disbelief)

RALPH: Yes, I would!

NORTON: So, what are you complaining about? You
GOT the little one!

**Conversation between Ralph Kramden and Ed Norton
in an episode of <u>The Honeymooners</u> (1955)**

CONTENTS

PREFACE

Since the publication of Roger Fisher and William Ury's highly influential book *Getting to Yes: Negotiating Agreement Without Giving In* (1981), it has been widely recognized that there is a middle ground—perhaps "high ground" would be better—between winning and losing in negotiations. Unlike *Getting to Yes*, however, which has helped disputants put some structure on their negotiation problem, our goal is to take such a well-structured problem and help the parties obtain a fair settlement. Thus, in a labor-management dispute, you certainly want to communicate clearly, to consider your opponent's interests as well as your own, and to persevere in taxing situations. But ultimately, you want to know on which issues you will win, on which you will lose, and on which you will have to compromise. By the same token, if you're facing a divorce, the question you want answered is, Who gets what?

This book presents new and superior procedures for helping the parties get to yes—if not nirvana—and most are not difficult to use. They take much of the worry out of being an inept bargainer by providing an ironclad guarantee of fairness. One of these step-by-step procedures even guarantees that the disputants will do as well as possible in realizing all the "win-win" potential that is available. Of course, sometimes there is no possibility of such mutual gain. If you are haggling with a car dealer, or your attorney is arguing the merits of an out-of-court settlement of your lawsuit, then any monetary gain for you is a loss for your opponent, and vice versa. The reader seeking clever advice on buying a car or settling a lawsuit can readily find it, but not here.

Our concern in this book is with disputes—from divorce to business to international—in which *everybody* can win. For such disputes, we will describe and illustrate step-by-step procedures that help the disputants resolve their differences, capture the mutual gain, and reach a fair settlement. But what does it mean to be "fair"? Isn't fairness—whatever it is—naive and out of fashion in this highly competitive world? Why shouldn't everyone go all out to win? Instead of compromising, isn't it better to be a tough negotiator and try to face down adversaries? Our answer is that "winning," at least in the all-out sense of beating an opponent, may not be in the cards. In fact, it is naive to think that the alternatives of being either a winner or a loser are the only ones. Typically, the real alternatives are that everybody can win (when negotiations succeed) or everybody can lose (when negotiations fail).

Our interest in fair division stems from a mathematical problem having its roots in the 1940s. Roughly speaking, the problem was whether the well-known two-person procedure of "I cut (a cake), you choose (a piece)," or divide-and-choose, can be extended to several people so as to ensure that everybody gets a piece that he or she considers to be at least as large as the pieces that other people receive. We solved this problem by finding such a procedure in 1992. This research, and related research on several other fair-division problems, are described in our book *Fair Division: From Cake-Cutting to Dispute Resolution* (1996), which was written for a theoretically oriented audience.

The present book takes a more practical view. We limit our discussion to a trio of procedures that can be easily implemented:

- Strict and balanced alternation (both based on taking turns);
- Divide-and-choose, and an extension called trimming; and
- Adjusted winner.

Strict alternation (first you choose an item, then I do, then you do, and so on) is as old as the hills, but what we do to make it fairer is new. This variant, called *balanced alternation*, is presented here for the first time and is especially applicable to disputes in which there are many items to be distributed, as one often finds in divorces and estate divisions. *Divide-and-choose* is well known and certainly not without its charms. While it goes back to the Hebrew Bible, it is seldom used today. The *trimming procedure* extends the idea underlying divide-and-choose to more than two parties. It was used, at least informally, to divide Germany and Berlin into four zones after World War II.

The last procedure, *adjusted winner*, is the centerpiece of the book and, we believe, has the greatest potential. But its use requires that the disputants think long and hard about how they value different items, and even what constitute "items." The product of these efforts is worth the cost: a settlement that has stronger claims to fairness than that provided by any of the other procedures in this book.

We keep the discussion relatively nontechnical throughout. Items set apart in the text, which provide elaborations of certain ideas, can be skipped on first reading. The sources and references at the end of the book provide details for the reader who wants to look further into the literature. Finally, a glossary gives definitions of important concepts, especially those that come up again and again in different contexts.

Besides our goals of describing different fair-division procedures and indicating in what situations they work best, we have a third, more ambitious goal: to help people settle their differences amicably. Toward this end, we offer numerous examples that illustrate how the various procedures may be applied to all kinds of conflicts, some hypothetical and some real. We believe the new procedures, especially, can help parties reduce the frustration, anger, and occasional violence that often accompany escalating demands and endless haggling. In the end, these procedures should enable parties to bring *their own* closure to a dispute, rather than have a settlement arbitrarily imposed on them or suffer from a continuing impasse.

ACKNOWLEDGMENTS

We thank Jon Hovi, Jeffrey R. Lax, Matthias G. Raith, and several anonymous reviewers of an earlier version of this book, who provided excellent comments. Early discussions with Arthur S. Goldberg and Daniel Candee were very fruitful. Finally, we had superb editorial help from our editor and the president of W. W. Norton, Drake McFeely, and the copy editor, Mary Babcock, for which we are grateful.

THE WIN-WIN SOLUTION

THE WIN-WIN SOLUTION

Chapter 1

INTRODUCTION

Disputes are nothing new, and neither is the idea of settling them fairly. To provide some historical perspective, let's look at some actual disputes and see how they were resolved, starting with contemporary ones and moving back to the Bible:

- The divorce of millionaire CEO Gary Wendt from his wife, Lorna Wendt;
- The settlement of French actor Yves Montand's estate via DNA testing of his exhumed corpse;
- The division of meat from a kill by African bushmen;
- The parceling out of territory by the Allies after World War II;
- The divvying up of pirates' treasure;
- The division of legislative powers in seventeenth-century England;
- The assessment of taxes, and the fabled division by animals of the returns from a hunt, in ancient Greece;
- King Solomon's proposed division of a disputed baby to establish maternity.

What distinguishes these cases is the use, or suggested use, of a dispute-resolution procedure—often based on some notion of fairness—rather than the arbitrary imposition of a settlement (though there is also some of this). Let's look at what procedures were employed in each of these cases.

FAIR-DIVISION STORIES

A CONTEMPORARY DIVORCE

In 1997, Gary C. Wendt, the chief executive officer of GE Capital Corporation, a profitable General Electric Company subsidiary, divorced his 54-year-old wife of 32 years, Lorna J. Wendt. Before the divorce, Gary's net worth was estimated to be about

$100 million, and Lorna sought a 50-50 split of the assets.

In January 1997, Lorna said, "This is not about need. I can get along on $10 million, but why should he get $90 million?" Indicating that it was not the money but the principle—that she had been a loyal corporate wife who had given up her career as a music teacher to rear the couple's two daughters, create an elegant home, give dinner parties for Gary's clients and co-workers, accompany him on business trips, and provide daily support in innumerable other ways to advance his career—Lorna added: "But I can turn it [Gary's claim to the lion's share] around and say, 'Well, what does he need all that money for?' He's out there working, and I've been fired." In court, Gary responded by saying that he was almost entirely responsible, by dint of his intelligence and hard work, for the creation of the Wendts' assets.

In December 1997, the judge in the divorce case awarded Lorna about $20 million of an estate now valued at $130 million. The explanation was that divorce law in Connecticut calls for equitable, not equal, distribution of the assets, leaving the judge free to consider the length of the marriage, the contributions that each partner had made to it, fault, need, and other circumstances. Customarily, judges in Connecticut mandate a 50-50 split only if the assets are worth less than $10 to $15 million, which was decidedly not true in the Wendt case. Because the judge disdained "judicial overreaching," he followed the usual practice of giving most of the remainder above the $10 to $15 million threshold to the breadwinner, who, as in the Wendt case, is usually the husband.

YVES MONTAND'S ESTATE

In 1989, a minor French actress, Anne-Gilberte Drossard, filed a paternity suit against the famous French actor, Yves Montand, alleging that he was the father of her child, Aurore Drossard, the result of a liaison she and Montand had had in the mid-1970s while they were working together on a film. Montand steadfastly denied that he was the father, but he died of a heart attack in 1991, at the age of 70, just three days before he was to testify in the trial.

In 1994, the French court ruled that Aurore was in fact Montand's daughter, in part because of a striking physical resemblance. But an appeal by Montand's family that included his two acknowledged children produced an order by the French Court of Appeals in the fall of 1997 to open Montand's tomb for a DNA test. The results of the test would determine not only whether Aurore would be able to share in Montand's estate, now valued at $3.7 million, but also how much of the total estate would be divided among her and Montand's two legitimate children.

The reason is that under French law, two children, whether legitimate or illegitimate, together inherit two-thirds of their parents' estate, but three children get three-fourths of it. However, a child born out of wedlock gets only half of the share of a child born in marriage. This stipulation would apply to Aurore, who was born in 1975 at the time of Montand's marriage to Simone Signoret, his wife of 36 years who died in 1985.

If Aurore were indeed Montand's child, she would be entitled to one-fifth of the 75% share of the three children, or 15%, whereas the two legitimate children would each be entitled to two-fifths of the 75% share, or 30% each. Thus, Aurore's entitlement would reduce the two legitimate children's share from 33.3% each to 30%.

In June 1998, the postmortem DNA tests showed that Aurore Drossard was not Yves Montand's daughter, reversing the earlier judgment of the Appeals Court. Even before the results were known, however, Aurore's grandmother, Anne Fleurange, charged that the tests would be inconclusive because the embalming formaldehyde made any analysis impossible.

BUSHMEN IN AFRICA

For thousands of years, hunting and gathering were practiced by all human beings. There is no formal record of how the resulting issues of fair division were handled, but some insights are provided by Elizabeth Marshall Thomas in her book, *The Harmless People* (1959).

In the 1950s, Thomas made several visits to study the Bushmen of southwestern Africa, the last significant population that still lived by hunting and gathering. While providing few details,

Thomas notes that the animals that were killed were "divided at once by a rigid system of rules." Continuing, she says, "It seems very unequal when you watch Bushmen divide a kill, yet it is their system, and in the end no person eats more than any other."

Although some tribesmen who take part in the kill *receive* more meat than others, they voluntarily share it with the others. In the end, Thomas points out, "It is not the amount eaten by any person but the formal ownership of every part that matters to Bushmen."

DIVISION OF TERRITORY AFTER WORLD WAR II

What procedures were employed when Allied leaders divided up territory at the end of World War II? Consider the following account of the deliberations between Winston Churchill and Joseph Stalin:

> As Churchill looked around the table at the opening session of the Tolstoy Conference in the Kremlin, at 10 P.M. on October 9, 1944, he decided the moment seemed "apt for business." "Let us settle our affairs in the Balkans," he began, in a phrase much quoted ever after. Then the prime minister wrote out his proposed arrangement on a sheet of plain paper. Russia should have 90 percent predominance in Rumania, Great Britain 90 percent in Greece. They would share fifty-fifty in Yugoslavia and Hungary, and Russia would have 75 percent predominance in Bulgaria. He pushed the paper across to Marshall Stalin who took a blue pencil, made a large tick upon it, and pushed it back.
>
> "After this there was a long silence," recalled Churchill. Finally, the prime minister spoke: "Might it not be thought rather cynical if it seemed we had disposed of these issues, so fateful to millions of people, in such an offhand manner? Let us burn the paper." "No, you keep it," replied Stalin.

The next day the bartering continued between Anthony Eden, the British foreign minister, and V. M. Molotov, the Soviet foreign minister:

> Molotov opened his conversation with Eden by stating that the fifty-fifty ratio proposed for Hungary was unacceptable. The Soviets wanted 75 percent. . . . He argued that Russia must have

90 percent influence . . . [in Bulgaria], as in Rumania. There followed in rapid succession a series of proposals, with Molotov at times offering to trade various percentages in Yugoslavia for near absolute control in Bulgaria and almost the same in Hungary. At one point he attempted to define what these numbers would mean. In Yugoslavia, said the Russian foreign minister, 60/40 meant that Britain would control the coast and Russia the center. Eden eventually agreed to what he thought was a decent compromise—a 20 percent share for Britain in Bulgaria and Hungary, reflected in a two-stage arrangement whereby after the war ended, Russia would allow an Allied control commission to function. For that, Molotov agreed to equal responsibilities in Yugoslavia. In all, the parceling out of the Balkans was at least reminiscent of the treatment of the Ottoman Empire after World War I, except that the stakes were people rather than oil.

It is difficult to find guiding principles behind these momentous decisions. While the divisions agreed to might reflect the interests of the dividers—who do indeed seem to be following some script, if not a procedure, in their exchanges—there is no apparent recognition of what leaders of the countries being carved up might desire.

PIRATES' TREASURE

Before pirates set out on a voyage, they would draw up a code of conduct that everyone was bound to observe, based on the principle "no prey, no pay." Once a ship was plundered, the captain received an agreed-upon amount for the ship plus a proportion of the cargo, which was measured by shares. But before shares were allocated, salaries were paid to the surgeon (200 to 250 pieces of eight) and the carpenter or shipwright, who mended and rigged the ship (100 to 150 pieces of eight). Next, money was given for recompense of injuries: 600 pieces of eight for loss of the right arm; 500 pieces of eight for loss of the left arm or right leg; 400 pieces of eight for loss of the left leg; and 100 pieces of eight for loss of an eye or a finger. After the disbursement of this medical insurance, the remaining loot was divided into shares, with the captain receiving five or six shares, the master's mate two shares, and the rest of the crew one share each. Any boys in the crew received half a share. It was a strict rule that no person should receive more than his proper due. Indeed, everyone had to take a solemn oath that they would not conceal and steal for themselves anything in a captured ship. There were severe penalties for disobedience.

PROPOSED CONSTITUTIONAL REFORM IN SEVENTEENTH-CENTURY ENGLAND

In the political arena, the English political theorist James Harrington, in a book called *The Commonwealth of Oceana* (1656), suggested a version of divide-and-choose that was intended to be a model for England. Harrington proposed a bicameral legislature in which an aristocratic Senate would, after debate, offer legislation (analogous to proposing a division of the cake), and a plebeian House, without debate, would vote on it (choose to pass it or not). A variation of this system, in which a committee can add and subtract provisions to a bill and a legislature can vote it up or down, is used in the U.S. Congress and many other legislatures today.

TAXATION IN ANCIENT GREECE

The idea of achieving fairness through procedures, as opposed to relying on the judgment of a leader, surfaces in ancient Greece about 600 B.C.E. in reference to a problem that persists today—property taxes. The solution inaugurated by the great Athenian statesman Solon, and used at the tribunals of Athens, was provided by the following procedure: Any citizen who thought that he was paying too high a property tax could exchange his property for that held by anyone who was paying less. While it's not clear how successful this switching possibility was in making tax assessments fair, proposing it today would surely introduce controversy into what might otherwise be a quiet town meeting.

AESOP'S FABLES

A lion, a fox, and an ass participated in a joint hunt. On request, the ass divided the kill into three equal shares and invited the others to choose. Enraged, the lion ate the ass and then asked the fox to make the division. The fox piled all the kill into one great heap except for one tiny morsel. Delighted at this division, the lion asked, "Who has taught you, my very excellent fellow, the art of division?" The fox replied, "I learnt it from the ass, by witnessing his fate."

A variation on this fable is that several animals find a treasure and must decide how to divide it fairly. The lion speaks up and says, "First, we must carefully divide the treasure into four parts. The first part goes to me, since I am king of the beasts. The second part is mine, owing to my strength. The third part is mine because of my courage. As for the fourth part, anyone who cares to dispute it with me can do so, at his own risk."

One may well applaud the fox for being a good learner in the first fable; in the second fable, one presumes that the other animals exhibited their erudition by remaining silent. While a fair-division procedure is ostensibly used in each of these fables, it is inherently corrupted by the lion's strength and reputation. Obviously, in situations in which there is a clear hierarchy, one is likely to get quick—but terribly unfair—resolutions that give the party at the top the "lion's share."

KING SOLOMON AND THE TWO MOTHERS

In the Hebrew Bible, the issue of fairness comes up frequently. For example, a first-born son is entitled to a double share of his father's estate (Deut. 21:17). While primogeniture is not justified in the Bible, to this day it remains a common custom in many societies.

Fairness issues also surface in some of the best-known biblical narratives. Cain's raging jealousy and eventual murder of Abel is provoked by what he considered unfair treatment by God, who "paid heed" to Abel's offering but ignored Cain's (Gen. 4:4). Jacob, after doing seven years of service in return for Laban's beautiful daughter, Rachel, was told that his sacrifice was not sufficient and that he had instead to marry Laban's older and plainer daughter, Leah, unless he did seven more years of service, which he regarded as not only the breaking of a contract but also blatantly unfair.

Fairness triumphed, however, when King Solomon proposed to divide a baby, claimed by two mothers, in two. When the true mother protested and offered the baby to the other mother, whose baby had died, the truth about the baby's maternity became apparent, and "all Israel . . . stood in awe of the king; for they saw that he possessed divine wisdom to execute justice" (1 Kings 3:28).

Solomon's proposed solution, however, is not really a procedure for fair division, because Solomon had no intention of dividing the baby in two. Instead, his purpose was more devious—to try to distinguish the true mother from the impostor.

The means used to settle disputes in all these cases are, in varying degree, *ad hoc*; certainly they are not well justified in terms of a method designed to produce certain ends. This is not to say that they are not practicable, and even acceptable, to the participants. Thus, for example, the pirates seem to have carefully thought out what each crew member, after a ship was plundered, was entitled to receive.

Similarly with Solomon: The situation he set up between the two mothers enabled him to interpret the strategies they chose, after announcing his own decision, as evidence of who was telling the truth and who was lying. In effect, he designed the rules in order to distinguish, based on the mothers' responses (protest or don't protest), truthfulness from mendacity.

Unfortunately, the pirates' and Solomon's rules of division relate only to their specific situations. How to generalize such rules to other situations is not evident. By contrast, our goal is to develop impartial rule-based procedures that provide a sturdier basis for making fair decisions than do the judgments of individuals (even a King Solomon!) or the judgments of collectivities like the pirates.

When a procedure is *perceived* to be fair because it satisfies certain criteria of fairness, it is more likely to lead to outcomes that are viewed as legitimate by all the parties. These outcomes will be more durable because, when seen as the product of a fair process, they are less likely to incite disaffected parties to try to derail them.

THE SETTING

Not every dispute will be suited to the procedures we discuss. Let's be more specific about the nature and kinds of disputes for which these procedures work.

TWO-PARTY DISPUTES

Two-party disputes are our focus; they are important for two reasons. First, many of the most intractable conflicts today, including divorces and labor-management disputes, inherently involve two parties. Still other conflicts, such as international disputes, often involve two coalitions whose members have shared interests and coordinate their actions. For all practical purposes, the coalitions can be considered two parties.

The second reason for concentrating on two party disputes is more practical. When there are three or more parties with distinct interests, the coalitional possibilities and cleavages increase rapidly, making a possible settlement not only more complicated but also less amenable to a procedural solution. Nevertheless, some of the most significant disputes in the world involve more than two parties, so we also discuss multiparty extensions of all the procedures.

GOODS AND ISSUES

The distinction between *goods*, such as the physical objects that must be divided among the heirs to an estate, and *issues*, which are matters on which there are opposing positions, such as the protectionist and free-trade positions in a trade dispute, is often blurry. Of course, many disputes, like divorce, involve both goods and issues.

What will be important in our later analysis is whether goods or issues, which we will refer to simply as *items*, are *divisible*— can they realistically be split or shared without losing their value?

One of the three procedures we discuss is designed for indivisible items, like the physical objects in a divorce, whereas the other two require that at most one item be divided, like land or even children (as in a joint-custody arrangement).

VOLUNTARY CHOICE

Underlying all our procedures is voluntary choice. A settlement is never imposed by an outside party, as is the case in arbitration. An *arbitrator*, by definition, makes an arbitrary—though presumably fair—decision that the disputants must accept.

Fair-division procedures, by contrast, leave to the disputants what choices they will make, as allowed by the rules. While arbitrators are excluded, there is a definite role for *mediators*, who may well serve as clarifiers and facilitators without dictating the settlement.

Thus, for example, mediators may help the disputants define what the issues are, including what needs to be divided, but not decide what the division will be. Typically, mediators ease communication, reduce tensions, and aid the disputants in working out practical details of applying specific procedures.

At a fundamental level, fairness is guaranteed by the procedure used, not the wisdom or benevolence of the mediator. This said, one must quickly ask the question: Are we assuming that each party will be completely honest and forthcoming? This is the question of *strategy*, which is discussed at length throughout the book.

PROCEDURES

Here is a quick overview of the three procedures that are described and illustrated in later chapters:

1. *Strict and balanced alternation. Strict alternation* is simply taking turns: You pick an item; then I pick one; you choose again; and so on. Of course, going first can be a huge advantage, and much of what is done later, including giving extra choices to compensate for going second, involves finding a reasonable way to reduce, if not eliminate, this advantage. That is, a specific way of balancing choices leads to a procedure called *balanced alternation*.

2. *Divide-and-choose.* This is the familiar "I cut, you choose" method, with which almost everybody has had some experience. What most people probably do not know is whether it is better to be the divider or the chooser. As we will see, it all depends on what the parties know about each other's preferences, as well as whether they wish to spite their opponents or think they might be spited themselves.

The *trimming procedure* extends divide-and-choose to more than two parties by requiring that, at different stages, they create equal shares for themselves. They do so by trimming what they consider to be the largest pieces to tie with smaller pieces, repeating the same procedure on the trimmings, the trimmings of the trimmings, and so on. Of course, this procedure can become very complicated, especially when there are many participants.

3. *Adjusted winner.* Under this procedure, the two parties begin by independently (that is, secretly) distributing a total of 100 points across all the items to be divided, depending on the relative value they attach to them. Thus, if you consider a certain item to be worth one-fourth of the total value of everything to be divided, then you would put 25 points on it.

The term *winner* in adjusted winner comes from the next step: Each party is (temporarily) given the items on which he or she placed more points than his or her opponent. Thus, if I place 24 points on the apartment and you place 25 points on it, you will get it, at least for the moment.

Now the *adjusted* part comes in: Suppose, initially, I win items totaling 55 of my points, and you win items totaling 65 of your points. Then we start transferring items from you to me, in a certain order, until the point totals are equalized (at, say, 60 points each). This order of transfer, which usually requires splitting one item, guarantees that the final allocation will satisfy some important properties of fairness.

STATING PREFERENCES

If a settlement is not to be imposed, then the parties must be given the opportunity to state their preferences, just as citizens

must be allowed to vote freely if a government is to be democratic. By contrast, with imposed settlements or under dictator-
ships, one is forced to rely on the wisdom or the good will of
someone else.

Without the participation of the disputants, or citizens in a
democracy, in the evaluation and selection process, this "solution" can produce arbitrary results. For democracies to work well,
many of us must be willing to vote by stating a preference for a
candidate or a political party. Analogously, for nonimposed fair
division to work well, disputants must be willing to indicate how
much they value certain things.

In terms of stating preferences, the least that a procedure can
ask is that the disputants be willing and able to pick a favorite
item. That is, given a collection of items, a disputant should be
able to point to one and say, "That item is at least as valuable to
me as any of the other items." This is all that is demanded, in fact,
by alternation procedures, making them especially easy to use.

With divide-and-choose, one must do more. For example, suppose that the other party has done the dividing, and now you
must do the choosing. This means that you have to compare two
collections of items and say which collection you prefer. This is
certainly harder than picking a single favorite item. Practically
speaking, of course, it is the dividing of these items into two collections, not the choosing of one, that may strain your ability to
make judgments.

Adjusted winner asks even more. After you distribute 100
points across all the items, based on their relative values, you
could, in theory, use these point allocations to split the items into
two piles, worth 50 points each, and use divide-and-choose. But
adjusted winner uses a different principle to construct two piles.
This principle requires that the parties indicate the relative value
of each item, not just construct two equal collections. Suffice it
to say that the dividends of using adjusted winner more than jus-
tify the additional effort needed to determine the relative values
of the items.

This, then, is our setting: a focus on two-party disputes, involving goods, issues, or both, and a consideration of procedures that

rely on voluntary choices and a willingness to state preferences and even quantify them. Our goal is to find procedures that enable each party to guarantee its own satisfaction, regardless of how the other party or parties behave or feel. But what does "satisfaction" mean, and how can it be guaranteed?

CRITERIA OF SATISFACTION

There are four criteria by which to judge the fairness of settlements. These will quickly reduce to three, because the first criterion is just a weaker version of the second and thus can be eliminated. A procedure is *fair* to the degree that it satisfies these criteria.

1. *Proportionality.* Satisfaction is linked, presumably, to receiving a "fair share." Although there are several criteria one might adduce to assess fairness, proportionality can be traced back to the Greek philosopher Aristotle, who argued in his book *Ethics* that goods should be divided in proportion to each claimant's contribution. For now, proportionality will arise only when contributions are equal. If there are two parties, *proportionality* will mean that each party thinks that it is getting at least one-half of the total value. If there are three parties, each thinks that it is getting at least one-third of the total value. And so on.

2. *Envy-Freeness.* What more than proportionality can one ask for? The answer is something called *envy-freeness*, which says that no party is willing to give up the portion it receives in exchange for the portion someone else receives. Hence, no party envies any other party.

   In two-party disputes, there is no difference between a proportional and an envy-free settlement. To see why this is so, assume a settlement is proportional, so you think you are getting at least one-half of the total value of all the items. Will you envy me? Of course not: If you think that you have at least one-half, then you must think that I have at most one-half. Symmetrically, if I think I have at least one-half, then I will not envy you, so the settlement is envy-free. Conversely, if the settlement is envy-free, then each of us must think that he or she is getting at least one-half; otherwise, at least one of us will envy the other for getting more than one-half. Thus, if there are only two parties, proportionality and envy-freeness are equivalent.

In the case of three parties, however, envy-freeness is stronger than proportionality. For example, I may think I'm getting one-third, but if I think you're getting one-half (because the third party, in my eyes, is getting only one-sixth), then I'll envy you. On the other hand, if an allocation among three parties is envy-free, then I must think I received at least one-third. (Otherwise, I would think the others together received more than two-thirds, and I would envy the one or both who received more than one-third.) Hence, an envy-free allocation is always proportional, even if there are more than two parties, but a proportional allocation is not necessarily envy-free.

3. *Equitability.* There is an aspect of satisfaction, related to envy-freeness, that is more subtle than envy-freeness. Think about a divorce settlement, in which you think you got 51% of the total value of the joint holdings but in which your spouse thinks he or she got 90% of the total value, because your spouse had little interest in what you got. Do you envy your spouse?

The answer is no. Assume the husband thinks he received 51%. Then regardless of what his wife thinks, in his eyes she received only 49% of the total value. But is he happy? Maybe, because he thinks he got the (slightly) bigger "half."

However, he probably will not be thrilled by the fact that his wife is a lot happier with what she got (90% in her view) than he is with what he got (51% in his view). Thus, while he does not envy her for what she received, he might well envy her greater happiness for having received much more of the total value in her view than he received of the total value in his view.

Equitability is used here to mean that both parties think they received the same fraction of the total, as each of them values the different items. Coupled with envy-freeness, it means not only that both get more than 50% but also that both exceed

50% by the same amount. For example, equitability would-hold if the husband believed he got 70% and his wife believed she got 70%, which is quite a different story from his believing that he got 51% and her believing that she got 90%. Clearly, when both spouses think they got 70% of the total value, they are equally pleased by their allocations.

Equitability may be a difficult property to ascertain. How does one measure whether both parties are equally happy with their allocations?

Fortunately, this assessment can be made with the point-allocation procedure, adjusted winner, in which each party distributes 100 points across the contested items in the dispute. The settlement will be equitable if party 1 receives the same value (as measured by its points) as party 2 does (as measured by its points).

4. *Efficiency.* Our final criterion for judging satisfaction is that there be no slack in the system that would enable more benefit to be spread around. A settlement is *efficient* if there is no other allocation that is better for some party without being worse for another party.

Efficiency by itself—that is, when not linked with properties like proportionality, envy-freeness, or equitability—is no guarantee that an allocation will be fair. For example, an allocation that gives everything to me and nothing to you is efficient: Any other allocation will make me worse off when it makes you better off. It is the other properties of fairness, combined with efficiency, that ensure that the total value is distributed to everyone's satisfaction.

We now have four properties for ascertaining whether parties are likely to be satisfied by a settlement: (1) proportionality, (2) envy-freeness, (3) equitability, and (4) efficiency. In the subsequent analysis, it is not necessary to assess fair-division procedures with respect to proportionality, because this property is implied by envy-freeness. On the other hand, the other three properties are independent of each other.

As we proceed, we will keep track of how our different fair-division procedures fare with respect to envy-freeness, equitability, and efficiency. When all is said and done, the fairness of a solution depends on the degree to which it satisfies these three properties.

These properties make little sense when there is no win-win potential. For example, if you are bargaining over the price of a car, what does it mean to say that the price is "envy-free"? The yardstick here, rather, is whether what you pay for the car is better than your BATNA (*B*est *A*lternative *T*o a *N*egotiated *A*greement), or fallback position. Your BATNA in this case might be the money you would have to put into the repair of your old car.

There is no obvious BATNA in the case of a divorce, a labor-management conflict, a clash between neighboring countries, and other disputes in which the two sides cannot simply walk away from the table. In the absence of a satisfactory alternative that each side can implement on its own, the disputants lack viable fallback positions. Therefore, each must determine what kind of *settlement* is minimally acceptable; washing one's hands of the other side is simply not an option.

A procedure that ensures a settlement's fairness, as measured by the properties of envy-freeness, equitability, and efficiency, is needed in situations in which the two sides have no recourse but to try to live—perhaps separated and with no communication, as in some divorces—with each other. The question then is: Which procedures work best in what situations? Additionally, how do they guarantee a fair settlement?

RULES AND STRATEGIES

Impartial procedures, which do not favor a particular party, are the key to finding a fair settlement of a dispute. A procedure is described by its rules, so let's be clear about what rules are.

Rules are legal choices that can be enforced by a referee, without knowledge of any party's preferences. Thus, a rule might say, "Divide the collection of items into two separate piles." By counting piles, a referee can tell whether this statement has been followed. But a rule cannot say, "Divide the collection of items into two separate piles that you consider to be equal in value," because a referee would have no way of knowing if the latter part of this statement were being followed.

Parties base their *strategies*, or courses of action, not only on the rules but also on their own private knowledge (for example, of the values of the different items). Once the rules have been laid down, there are many possible strategies that parties can select. For example, if you are the divider in divide-and-choose, then one rule says that you must divide the items into two piles. The added phrase "that you consider to be of equal value" is a strategy that provides a certain kind of guarantee, as we will see.

Nothing says that you must use the prescribed strategy. In fact, we will see later that there are situations in which you might want to deviate from such a strategy, based on information you have about how your opponent values the different items.

So why is the strategy of equal division in divide-and-choose a good one? The answer is that it provides you with a guarantee of a certain kind of satisfaction—in this case, envy-freeness. We call such a strategy a *guarantee strategy*, because the satisfaction you derive from using it does not depend on the actions of others. As we will see later, however, divide-and-choose can result in an allocation that is quite inequitable and far from efficient.

Departing from a guarantee strategy is often ill-advised. Solomon's deception is a case in point. If he had failed to outwit the impostor with his subterfuge, and she had protested too, Solomon might well have had to carry out his edict to divide the baby in two, which would not have sent his reputation soaring. True, there are less radical solutions that Solomon might have tried, such as removing the baby from both mothers had they not been able to reach an agreement on their own. But this kind of solution is beyond the scope of our study, which precludes an outside party from influencing how a fair division will be made.

Our goal is to find procedures, governed by rules, that the disputants themselves can implement. Associated with these rules will be strategies that the disputants can use to guarantee themselves a certain degree of satisfaction. The combination of rules and strategies, and how they might best be applied, are our main concerns in the rest of the book.

The idea of replacing the judgment of an outside party, when possible, by procedures with some claim to impartiality has been championed by economics Nobel laureate Herbert A. Simon. In his autobiography, *Models of My Life* (1991), Simon says:

> The distribution of the world's goods owes little to virtue. . . . There must be better games. If I were to select a research problem without regard to scientific feasibility, it would be that of finding how to persuade human beings to design and play games that all can win.

Simon's "games that all can win" necessarily have rules. Indeed, they are tantamount to the procedures, to be discussed in the following chapters, that give everybody a fair shake.

Chapter 2
STRICT ALTERNATION

Ann and Ben are getting a divorce and must divide up the following three big items:

- A four-bedroom house;
- A retirement account (pension), which, though substantial, will remain untouchable for several years; and
- A portfolio of investments, which has lower monetary value than the pension but is all liquid assets.

In addition to these, they must resolve the question of the custody of their 12-year-old daughter, Carol. Not surprisingly, neither is willing to see "custody" listed as an item if losing means having one's visitation rights at the complete discretion of an ex-spouse. Joint custody, on the other hand, is not a viable option, because Ann and Ben will be living in different school districts.

Fortunately, reason has prevailed, and both parents have agreed that "winning" on the issue of custody means primary custody in the sense that Carol will attend school in the district in which that parent lives, with the other parent having Carol for school vacations, including the summer. Both Ann and Ben feel they can live with a loss on this issue if such a loss comes as part of a *package* that represents a "fair settlement" of the divorce.

TAKING TURNS

Perhaps the most common way for two people like Ann and Ben to divide a collection of items is to take turns, whereby first one person chooses an item, then the other, and so on. Assume, for the moment, that Ann goes first as the result of the toss of a coin, so the choice sequence they use for the four items (including custody) is Ann-Ben-Ann-Ben.

This sequence is called *strict alternation*. Not only do the parties alternate, but each selects only one item when it is his or her turn to choose. When one party can select more than one item when it is his or her turn to choose, alternation is not strict.

Suppose Ann and Ben rank the four items from best (rank 1) to worst (rank 4) as follows:

Rank	Ann	Ben
1	Pension	House
2	House	Investments
3	Investments	Custody
4	Custody	Pension

Suppose, further, that they make *sincere choices*: Each person selects his or her favorite item from among those remaining at each stage. Then Ann will choose the pension and Ben will choose the house, after which Ann will choose the investments and Ben will get primary custody of Carol. Thus, Ann will get her first and third choices, which is not unexpected since she is choosing first and third.

But what if Ann knows Ben's preferences and seeks to capitalize on this knowledge? Ann could then begin not by selecting the pension, in which Ben has little interest, but instead by choosing the house. Her hope, of course, is that the pension will still be available for her after Ben makes his first choice.

This is a bit of a gamble on Ann's part. To be sure, Ben prefers the investments to the pension and so, if he is looking out for his own good, would choose the investments. This way, Ann might surmise, she would get the pension (her top choice) on her final turn, giving her the pension and house, which are her top two choices.

So why is this a gamble for Ann? For one thing, she may not be sure of Ben's preferences. But even if she is, another factor comes into play—spite. If Ben sees through what Ann is doing, he may well look beyond the allocation of these four items in deciding which object he should select when his turn comes up.

Indeed, it is not uncommon in divorces that one party, when purposefully put in an inferior position by the other party, will settle for less in material terms in order to "get even." The husband, for example, might prefer the satisfaction of denying his wife what she most wants by "getting back" at her for trying to be exploitative or manipulative.

Emphatically, this choice is not irrational. In fact, teaching Ann that she cannot get away with this kind of manipulation may, in the long run, benefit Ben in tangible as well as intangible ways. Thus, if Ann and Ben are likely to have extended future negotiations—for example, involving their daughter, Carol—Ben may well want to send a strong message that he is no patsy.

THE BOTTOM-UP STRATEGY

Having illustrated the possibilities of manipulation in a simple example, let's find out if there is any systematic way of analyzing the best strategic choices that two parties can make. For the moment, we'll assume that both parties know each other's preferences, which is by no means always the case. We'll also assume that each knows that the other will act *rationally*, without spite, in terms of his or her own interests. Exactly what will rational parties do?

It is natural to assume that rational parties will

1. Never choose their least-preferred item;
2. Not "waste" choices on a desired item that they know will remain available and, hence, can be chosen later.

To illustrate the effects of these assumptions, let's return to our previous example with Ann and Ben and the four items they have to divide up. Ann's decision to pass over her top choice (the pension) on the first round was based on an informal mental calculation suggesting that it would still be available for her to take with her next choice, assuming that Ben did not choose to spite her.

To make such a mental calculation more precise, think about how Ann would reason to decide what her first choice should be. She knows that the eventual choice sequence will fill in the following blanks:

	First choice	Second choice	Third choice	Fourth choice
Ann:	_____		_____	
Ben:		_____		_____

Working backward from right to left, Ann first puts herself in Ben's shoes and asks what his *last* choice will be. The answer is that Ben's last choice will be the bottom item on *Ann's list*—namely, custody. That is, Ben knows that Ann will never choose her least-preferred item (according to assumption 1 above and our assumption that Ben *knows* that Ann is rational, and so he will never waste an earlier choice on it, according to assumption 2 above). Hence, Ann can pencil in "custody" as *Ben's* last choice:

	First choice	Second choice	Third choice	Fourth choice
Ann:	_____		_____	
Ben:		_____		Custody

(Actually, for Ann to pencil in this choice for Ben, it is not enough for *her to know* that Ben is rational. She must also know *that Ben knows* that *she* is rational.)

A completely analogous line of reasoning shows that Ben will never choose *his* least preferred item (the pension), and so Ann will wait until her last choice to take it. Thus, we can next pencil in "pension" for Ann:

	First choice	Second choice	Third choice	Fourth choice
Ann:	_____		Pension	
Ben:		_____		Custody

With custody and the pension eliminated from consideration, Ann can assume that she and Ben will reason as if these items never existed. For the remaining two items, the choice sequence is Ann-Ben. Again, Ann pencils in items from right to left, assuming that Ben will work from the bottom to the top of *her* list. This yields the next choice:

	First choice	Second choice	Third choice	Fourth choice
Ann:	_____		Pension	
Ben:		Investments		Custody

And, finally, the only remaining choice must go to Ann:

	First choice	*Second choice*	*Third choice*	*Fourth choice*
Ann:	House		Pension	
Ben:		Investments		Custody

Remember that this is just a mental calculation that Ann went through in order to decide what she will choose first (the house). Ann has no guarantee that Ben will, in fact, respond by selecting the investments next, as indicated.

Nevertheless, there is more than intuition to back up this *bottom-up strategy*, which leads to what are called *sophisticated choices*. In 1971, two mathematicians, D. A. Kohler and R. Chandrasekaran, proved that the bottom-up strategy is *optimal* in the sense that if you know your opponent is using it, you can do no better than use it yourself. In other words, if both parties use it, neither would have any reason to deviate from it, making these choices stable against each other.

Relying on an opponent to respond in a way that is at once sophisticated and without spite is, of course, a risky business. Perhaps a better way to view the bottom-up strategy is as a new procedure, implemented by a referee to whom the parties submit their rankings of all the items. Unfortunately, this procedure itself can be manipulated, as we can see from our previous four-item example:

Rank	*Ann*	*Ben*
1	Pension	House
2	House	Investments
3	Investments	Custody
4	Custody	Pension

In this example, the bottom-up strategy gave Ann her top two choices (pension and house), whereas Ben got only his second and third choices (investments and custody).

But now suppose that Ben had lied and submitted a ranking identical to Ann's. Then the bottom-up strategy would give Ann the pension and investments, and Ben the house and custody. While it seems that Ben is getting his second and fourth choices, in reality they are his first and third choices, as seen from the table that gives his true rankings. Hence, Ben's lying pays off: He improves his collection by replacing a second choice (the investments) with a first choice (the house) without changing the second item (custody) that he also receives.

Thus, there is an optimal strategy (the bottom-up strategy) that can be used if both parties have knowledge of each other's preferences. It can also be used by a referee, to whom the two parties submit their rankings of items. However, an insincere submission can be beneficial to a party, even though the bottom-up choices of both parties are stable against each other.

ASSESSMENT

Let's return to our criteria for evaluating fair-division procedures, applying them to strict alternation.

ENVY-FREENESS

Strict alternation can create envy, even when only item-by-item comparisons are made. For example, Ben will definitely envy Ann if she goes first, the number of items is even, and they rank the items the same. This is because Ann will get the preferred of their two highest-ranked items, the preferred of their two next-highest ranked items, and so on.

EFFICIENCY

Recall from Chapter 1 what it means to say that an allocation is *not* efficient: There is another allocation in which some party is better off and no party is worse off. Thus, the question of efficiency involves asking the parties to compare not just individual items but collections—sets of items they receive from one allocation versus those they receive from another.

In fact, though, an important feature of strict alternation is that parties never have to compare collections—the allocation requires only item-by-item comparisons. The ability to make item-by-item comparisons, however, translates into an ability to say that some collections are preferred to others by a party. For example, if Ann prefers

- The pension to the house, and
- The investments to custody,

then she certainly prefers the collection consisting of the pension and the investments to the collection consisting of the house and custody.

If we also presume that a new item added to a collection only makes that collection more desirable, then Ann would also prefer the collection consisting of the pension and investments *and* some other item to the collection consisting of just the house and custody. In situations like this, we say that the former collection is *item-by-item preferred* (by one of the parties) to the latter collection.

Under the assumption that the parties can only compare collections if one collection is item-by-item preferred to another, it is easy to show that strict alternation is efficient if

- Both parties are sincere by choosing the best item available; or
- Both parties use the bottom-up strategy.

In the case of sincere strategies, however, a deviation by one party can result in a better allocation for that party (but at the expense of the other). Thus, in our earlier example involving a house, investments, pension, and custody, Ann benefited by skipping over her first choice, the pension, and choosing her second choice, the house, at the start.

In the case of bottom-up strategies, by contrast, if one party effects a different allocation by a single unilateral deviation from the bottom-up strategy—but follows this strategy in choosing all other items—then the deviating party will not only fail to do better in an item-by-item comparison but will actually do worse. Thus in our earlier example, Ann would do worse by (sincerely) choosing the pension rather than skipping to her second choice of the house.

Instead of assuming that only item-by-item comparisons can be made, let's now assume that any two collections can be compared. Then efficiency can fail. For example, suppose that there are six items that Ben considers to be almost equally valuable. Ann, by contrast, thinks two are of about equal value and the other four are virtually worthless.

Then *both* Ann and Ben will prefer the result given by the choice sequence Ann-Ann-Ben-Ben-Ben-Ben to the result given by strict alternation. The former will give Ann nearly 100% of what she wants, and Ben about 67%, whereas strict alternation would give Ann only 50% of what she wants (if Ben, at the beginning, takes one of her two preferred items) and Ben only about 50% (by leaving him with only three items rather than four).

Thus, whether or not strict alternation is efficient depends very much on what assumptions we make about the parties' ability to compare collections. The procedure is efficient, based on item-by-item comparisons, if the parties make either sincere or sophisticated choices. But there may be other choice sequences that benefit both parties when, without being restricted to making item-by-item comparisons, they compare entire collections.

EQUITABILITY

This property is difficult to interpret in the case of strict alternation. Take the earlier example in which Ann and Ben must divide up a house, investments, and a pension (ignoring the custody issue for now). If Ben rather than Ann goes first, the sincere and sophisticated choices coincide—Ben gets the house and investments, whereas Ann gets the pension. One might ask, Is the allocation of the house and the investments to Ben (his first two choices), and the pension to Ann (her first choice), equitable?

Because we do not know what fraction of the total value Ben thinks the house and investments represent, and what fraction Ann thinks the pension represents, we cannot say whether or not their fractional shares of the total value are the same. But what we can say in this case is the minimum that each person must receive.

Specifically, because Ben ranks the house and the investments number one and two, he must think that he gets at least two-thirds of the total value—his last choice, the pension, cannot be worth more than one-third. By comparison, assume Ann thinks her top choice, the pension, is worth barely more than one-third of the total value. Then she may end up with only about one-third of the total, as she values the items, compared with the two-thirds (or more) that Ben thinks he receives.

Surprisingly, Ann could actually do better than Ben, comparatively speaking, if she thinks that the pension is worth more than two-thirds of the total value, and Ben values all the items about the same (so he gets only about two-thirds from the two he obtains). Thus, one cannot say much about equitability on the basis of the rankings alone.

EXTENSIONS TO THREE OR MORE PARTIES

Strict alternation, by its very nature, gives an advantage to the person choosing first, as we have seen. This advantage is apparent when there are only two items, and one person (say, Ann) goes first and can choose her favorite item. If this item is also Ben's favorite, then he does worse than Ann, even in his own terms, so this division is not envy-free. If we add a third item and a third person who chooses last, and her preferences are the same as those of the other two people, then she will do the worst of all three, envying Ben as well as Ann.

There are situations in which it is reasonable to give a break to certain parties, such as teams in a professional sports league that finished poorly during the season. To make these teams more competitive in the next season, some professional sports, like football, give them the first choice among the new players who come out of a pool called the *draft*.

Typically, the team with the worst win-loss record gets the first pick in the draft; the team with the next-worst record, the second pick; and so on. Selections continue, round after round, in this order until the draft choices of all teams are exhausted.

This procedure would seem fair in balancing the needs of the teams and the needs of the professional sport. A professional sports organization wants to make competition close and exciting, because this will enhance spectator interest, resulting in greater revenues for all teams. The teams, on the other hand, want to choose the best draft players available in order to maximize their own chances of making the playoffs and winning a championship.

In extending strict alternation to three or more parties, it is no longer correct to say that the parties "alternate" (first one chooses, then the other), because now there is more than one "other." Thus, we will switch to the terminology of *taking turns*, which was introduced earlier, whereby each of three or more parties will have a first turn before it takes a second turn, a second turn before it takes a third turn, and so on.

When there are more than two parties, sincere choices become even more vulnerable to strategic manipulation than they were in the case of two parties. To illustrate this point with an example, consider what sincere choices would yield three football teams, Atlanta, Baltimore, and Chicago, when there are six players: a center, a guard, a tackle, a quarterback, a halfback, and a fullback. Assume they are to be chosen in two rounds, and the rankings of these players by the teams (from most desired at the top to least desired at the bottom) are as follows:

Atlanta	*Baltimore*	*Chicago*
Center	Halfback	Tackle
Guard	Fullback	Fullback
Tackle	Guard	Halfback
Quarterback	Center	Quarterback
Halfback	Quarterback	Center
Fullback	Tackle	Guard

Rankings

If Atlanta chooses first, Baltimore second, and Chicago third, then the results of their sincere selections—round by round (top choices first round, lower choices second round)—are especially good for Atlanta and Baltimore. They get their two most-preferred players (underscored), as depicted on the next page.

Atlanta	Baltimore	Chicago
Center	Halfback	Tackle
Guard	Fullback	Fullback
Tackle	Guard	Halfback
Quarterback	Center	Quarterback
Halfback	Quarterback	Center
Fullback	Tackle	Guard

Sincere Choices

Even Chicago does not do too badly, getting its first and fourth choices (notice that its second and third choices, the halfback and the fullback, are taken by Baltimore before Chicago selects a second player).

It is not difficult to show that sincere choices like these are *always* efficient, even when there are more than two teams: There is no other assignment that would help *all* the teams in an item-by-item comparison. This result is apparent in our example, in which Atlanta and Baltimore get their top two choices. In order to improve on this result, one would have to find an assignment of players in which Atlanta and Baltimore continue to get their top two choices and Chicago also does better. But this is obviously impossible because, after Atlanta and Baltimore receive their top two choices, only the tackle and the quarterback are unassigned, and they must go to Chicago.

The strategic problem with these sincere choices is that the teams have an incentive to depart from them (see "Logic of Optimal Departures," below). This logic gives the following optimal choices (underscored) for all three teams:

Atlanta	Baltimore	Chicago
Center	Halfback	Tackle
Guard	Fullback	Fullback
Tackle	Guard	Halfback
Quarterback	Center	Quarterback
Halfback	Quarterback	Center
Fullback	Tackle	Guard

Sophisticated Choices

As in the two-party case, these choices are called *sophisticated*, and the resulting assignment of choices to the teams is the *sophisticated outcome*.

LOGIC OF OPTIMAL DEPARTURES

Assume that Atlanta first considers the possibility of selecting its top choice (the center). If Baltimore then selects its own top choice (the halfback), then Chicago will definitely bypass the tackle and take the fullback—lest Baltimore take the fullback on the second round—which will result in the following allocation of players (all teams can do no better than choose sincerely on the second round):

- Atlanta gets the center and the guard;
- Baltimore gets the halfback and the quarterback;
- Chicago gets the tackle and the fullback.

Thus, Chicago gets its two top choices.

Anticipating that Chicago will make the strategic choice of the fullback if Baltimore is sincere, Baltimore asks what will happen if it selects, say, the guard instead of the halfback during the first round. In this case, Chicago can do no better than select the tackle, resulting in the following allocation of players:

- Atlanta gets the center and the quarterback;
- Baltimore gets the guard and the halfback;
- Chicago gets the tackle and the fullback.

This represents an improvement for Baltimore.

So far, we have seen that if Atlanta is sincere, then Baltimore does better by selecting the guard rather than the halfback during the first round. Similar arguments can be used to show that Baltimore, in fact, always does better by choosing the guard during the first round than by making any other choice. Thus, Atlanta knows that if it is sincere with its first choice, then the final allocation will give it the center and the quarterback.

In a similar fashion (yes, some complications are being left out here), Atlanta can determine exactly what the final allocation will be if it selects the guard as its first choice or, for that matter, any other player. If we compare these allocations, then it turns out that the best choice for Atlanta is to select the tackle (its third choice) during the first round, resulting in the following allocations of players:

- Atlanta gets the center and the tackle;
- Baltimore gets the halfback and the guard;
- Chicago gets the fullback and the quarterback.

Comparing these choices with the earlier sincere choices, we see that *all* three teams do worse by acting sophisticatedly. This is evident in the case of Atlanta and Baltimore, each of which gets its top two choices when the teams are sincere and its first and third choices when they are sophisticated. Chicago also prefers the sincere outcome, which gives it the tackle instead of the fullback (in both the sincere and sophisticated allocations, Chicago obtains the quarterback). Thus, player-by-player, each team gets either the same or a more-preferred player when all the teams' choices are sincere rather than sophisticated.

In sum, when each team follows an individually optimal choice strategy based on the sophisticated calculations illustrated in "Logic of Optimal Departures," the resulting outcome hurts everybody. This is a three-person incarnation of the infamous two-person Prisoners' Dilemma in game theory, which was the name coined for this game in the 1950s (see "Story of Prisoners' Dilemma," next page).

In the case of Prisoners' Dilemma, two prisoners who make the rational choice of confessing do worse than if they had both remained silent. Likewise in the football draft, three or more teams can hurt themselves by making sophisticated choices rather than sincere choices. This bizarre fact has been called the *paradox of player selection*. Other forms of competition—in a developing country, having more children; in a business, lowering the price of a product—also have the earmarks of a Prisoners' Dilemma. Overpopulation in the developing country, and unprofitable prices in the business, wreak havoc on everyone involved. But each parent and each business has a clear incentive to act in this unproductive way, regardless of what the others do.

How might the paradox of player selection be avoided? It is probably impossible to dictate to teams that they make sincere choices in order to ensure an efficient outcome. Notice, in the case of the sophisticated outcome, that it is only Atlanta's first choice of the tackle that is insincere—the teams choose sincerely thereafter. Yet if Atlanta were to make its first choice sincerely by selecting the center, Baltimore and Chicago would be in a position to gain by being insincere themselves.

One possible way to ensure efficiency is to arrange for trades to restore efficiency after the draft, but it turns out that the only trade that does this in the football example is a three-way cyclical trade, with the tackle going to Chicago, the fullback to Baltimore, and the guard to Atlanta. This trade, moreover, cannot be effected by a sequence of mutually advantageous two-way trades, because the player that each team wants is not held by the team that desires the player it holds. In fact, no mutually advantageous two-way trade is possible from the sophisticated outcome.

STORY OF PRISONERS' DILEMMA

Two people suspected of being partners in a crime are arrested and placed in separate cells so that they cannot communicate with each other. Without a confession from at least one suspect, the district attorney does not have sufficient evidence to convict them of the crime. In an attempt to extract a confession, the district attorney tells each suspect the following consequences of their (joint) actions:

1. If one suspect confesses and the other one does not, the one who confesses can go free for cooperating with the state, but the other suspect gets a stiff ten-year sentence.
2. If both suspects confess, both get reduced sentences of five years.
3. If both suspects remain silent, both go to prison for one year on the lesser charge of carrying a concealed weapon.

What should the suspects do to save their own skins, assuming that neither has any compunction against "squealing" on the other? Observe, first, that if one suspect confesses, it is advantageous for the other to do likewise and get five years rather than the worse outcome of ten years in prison. On the other hand, if the first suspect does not confess, it is still better for the other suspect to turn state's evidence by confessing and, therefore, to go free rather than spend one year in prison. Hence, <u>whatever the first suspect does</u>, the other one always does better by confessing, making this the rational choice. The same argument, of course, applies to the first suspect.

The rub is that both suspects, following this logic, will confess, so both receive sentences of five years. On the other hand, if both remained silent, both would get only one year in prison, which is better for both of them—yet not a rational choice since squealing always gets them a preferred outcome (less jail time).

A three-way cyclical trade would probably be difficult to find, much less arrange, in most fair-division problems. Thus, "trading up to efficiency" seems to be a rather impractical way to repair the damage wrought by parties that, once they lose their innocence, act sophisticatedly.

A surprising feature of the foregoing example is that Atlanta and the other two teams do better when Atlanta chooses last rather than first; the order of the other two teams does not affect the outcome. In fact, the sophisticated outcome when Atlanta chooses last is the same as the sincere outcome. These choices (underscored) coincide with the sincere outcome, shown earlier, when Atlanta chooses first:

Baltimore	Chicago	Atlanta
Halfback	Tackle	Center
Fullback	Fullback	Guard
Guard	Halfback	Tackle
Center	Quarterback	Quarterback
Quarterback	Center	Halfback
Tackle	Guard	Fullback

Sincere and Sophisticated Choices

This result has been called the *paradox of team position*, because one would expect that a team would find it counterproductive to give up its first pick in the draft. But precisely the opposite happens: Atlanta, as well as Baltimore and Chicago, all end up with a better set of players when Baltimore goes first, Chicago second, and Atlanta last, and all the teams make sophisticated choices (which happen also to be sincere in this case). Strangely, then, the team choosing first (Atlanta) may beg to be allowed to choose last, and it may be to the advantage of the other teams to support Atlanta's entreaty.

There is no known simple rule, like that of the bottom-up strategy in the two-party case, for finding sophisticated outcomes when there are more than two teams making selections, as in professional football. The fact that the sophisticated outcome (1) will not always be efficient, (2) cannot be easily made so with simple trades, (3) does not necessarily favor the first chooser, and (4) is not necessarily unique (this is not difficult to show) calls into question whether this outcome would be what three or more parties would want of a fair-division procedure—assuming that a priority list, giving the order of choice by the teams, could be agreed to by the teams.

In many situations, of course, one does not want to set priorities, as when all children are considered equal beneficiaries of an estate. Thus, if some form of taking turns is to be used, the problem is not to build in priorities but to take them out.

RECOMMENDATIONS

For many of us, an early lesson in fair division occurred in elementary school with the choosing of sides for a spelling bee, or the choosing of members of a team for a ball game on the playground. In terms of importance, of course, the choices that children make pale in comparison with those made by spouses when they must divide up the marital property in a divorce. Remarkably, however, strict alternation is frequently used in both situations—not to mention many other situations, like estate division, that may involve more than two parties.

What is it about strict alternation that commends it for such widespread use? The answer seems to be that it scores high marks on two important criteria:

1. Asking little of participants in terms of the statements they must make regarding their preferences;
2. Being simple to understand, with its claims to fairness quite apparent.

Strict alternation, nevertheless, has two significant flaws, the first of which is the envy that it may generate. Even if one flips a coin to decide who has the right to choose first, the first chooser may be strikingly and permanently advantaged. This bias, determined solely by luck, seriously undermines the fairness of taking turns, except in situations like a professional sports draft in which one *wants* certain teams to be advantaged (though this may not always be the case if they are sophisticated, as we have seen).

The second major flaw with strict alternation is that it is efficient only in the weak sense of item-by-item comparisons. In many situations, people will be both willing and able to make comparisons of collections of items, not just their components, and these comparisons will reveal the inefficiency of strict alternation.

In fairness to strict alternation, however, efficiency—in the strong sense of comparing collections—is only rarely achieved. The exception will come with our third procedure, adjusted winner, which satisfies all three criteria of fairness. But using adjusted winner requires that the parties reveal more information about their preferences—not just indicate a preferred item at each step.

Strict alternation has some merit, especially in sports drafts in which one *wants* to create certain biases in the procedure. In theory, choices can be manipulated strategically, but the calculations are very complicated, even assuming that the parties know each others' preferences. Not only are these calculations probably not worth the effort, but also everybody can lose in the end, as we saw.

For two equally deserving parties, there is no excuse for not trying to compensate the party choosing second in a way that ameliorates the problem of envy. It is only when both parties think all the items are roughly equal in value—so nobody is likely to be aggrieved by the order of choice—that the simplicity of strict alternation makes it an attractive procedure.

Chapter 3
BALANCED ALTERNATION

We know from Chapter 2 that strict alternation can give a big boost to the first chooser when there are only two parties. What we need to do is to reduce this advantage of the first chooser by amending strict alternation. A new procedure, called *balanced alternation,* allows the parties to take turns to be the first chooser at different points in the selection process.

But let's first dispose of items over which there is no conflict, which greatly simplifies the task of reaching a fair settlement under any alternation procedure. This step reduces the conflict to just the items that are *contested*—that both parties want during the same round—and in a way makes it possible for both parties to go first, with each getting what it wants at the same time.

THE QUERY STEP

We return to the divorce example described in Chapter 2, in which Ann ranks the pension first and Ben ranks the house first. In this case, we simply give the pension to Ann and the house to Ben and move on to other items, since their two top-ranked choices are not in conflict.

Notice that, in terms of indicating preferences, this step requires nothing more of each spouse than to indicate a single favorite item from the collection of items. If, as in our example, each indicates a different item, the division of the rest of the property can proceed as if neither the pension nor the house were part of the settlement—each has already been allocated.

If the two spouses want the same item at the start, place it in a *contested pile.* The selection process then continues. Once again, ask each spouse to designate his or her favorite item from those that remain—that is, from among the items that (1) have not yet been awarded to either party and (2) have not yet been placed in the contested pile. The sequence of questions that leads to allocating different items to Ann and Ben, or placing items they both want in the contested pile, is called the *query step*.

It may sound as if the query step requires an arbitrator or mediator: Such a person asks Ann which item she most prefers and, independently, asks Ben which item he most prefers. Then either both items are awarded, or the item is contested and placed in the contested pile. In fact, however, an arbitrator or mediator is not needed: Ann and Ben can simply write down their preferred choices, in secret, on a slip of paper and, simultaneously, reveal them.

Repeated over and over again, Ann and Ben at each stage will choose two different items, or will choose the same item, which will then be placed in the contested pile. Notice that if there are eight items, for example, then the actual number of questions that need to be asked in order to divide all the items is between four and seven:

- Four if the items are never contested (two will be allocated at each stage);
- Seven if the items are always contested (none will be allocated at each stage; the last item will necessarily be contested, so an eighth question need not be asked).

An important consequence of using the query step is that there will be complete agreement between Ann and Ben on the ranking, from best to worst, of items in the contested pile. Their top-ranked item in this pile will be the first that was put there; the second-ranked item will be the next that was put there; and so on.

Thus, we have reduced the fair-division problem to one of allocating only the items in the contested pile in which the two parties each have the same most-preferred item, next most-preferred item, and so on down to a common least-preferred item. Assuming the parties do not change their preferences as a result of the allocation of the uncontested items, they will contest each and every item in the contested pile.

In this situation, unlike several of the examples in Chapter 2, the parties cannot benefit from making insincere choices.

Consequently, under strict alternation, their optimal choices of items in the contested pile will always be sincere.

TAKING TURNS TAKING TURNS TAKING TURNS . . .

The query step and the contested pile remove the problem of the parties' making insincere choices from the contested pile. But we know from Chapter 2 that strict alternation may be unfair even with sincere choices. So let's consider some variants of strict alternation. Suppose that there are four items to be divided in the contested pile, and assume that Ann goes first. Other than strict alternation (Ann-Ben-Ann-Ben), there are two natural sequences:

- Ann-Ben-Ben-Ann
- Ann-Ben-Ben-Ben

Both of these are alternating procedures that make up, in a way, for Ann's advantage as the first chooser. Ben receives compensation, in effect, by being able to choose more than one item—after Ann does—when it is his turn to choose.

Patently, the roles of the two parties are even less symmetric than under strict alternation. This added asymmetry may evoke bad feelings, regardless of what the outcome is, if one party thinks his or her opponent is favored by the procedure.

Indeed, it is not at all clear in our example whether Ben needs two choices in a row, or three, to catch up to Ann, even if the parties like exactly the same items, and in the same order. In fact, it is easy to think of situations in which even three choices in a row would not be sufficient to achieve fairness. For example, if the items to be divided are a sports car, a bedside table, a clock, and a lamp, would you really want to be Ben in the Ann-Ben-Ben-Ben sequence?

ADDRESSING THE FIRST-CHOOSER PROBLEM:
TWO TURNS

Let's begin by considering the simplest possible fair-division problem, that in which there is only one item in the contested pile. If Ann chooses first, she receives it, so Ben is left with nothing. With two items, the situation is not much better: Ann gets the preferred item, and Ben the nonpreferred item, if they continue to rank the items the same. In both of these cases, there is not much we can do except recognize the limitations, or inappropriateness, of an alternating procedure. True, its arbitrariness can be reduced by using a random device to determine who goes first, but this makes who is advantaged simply a matter of luck.

Remarkably, though, if there are several items (for concreteness, assume there are four), then the advantage held by the party going first can be diminished by an alternating procedure's fundamental tenet: taking turns. To be more precise, a basic step in alternation can be thought of as being one of two different kinds:

1. *An Ann-first step*: Ann chooses one item, then Ben does.
2. *A Ben-first step*: Ben chooses one item, then Ann does.

Clearly, an Ann-first step favors Ann, whereas a Ben-first step favors Ben. In either case, we call such alternation *taking turns*.

Fairness considerations suggest that we take turns using Ann-first steps and Ben-first steps. Notice that with four items, an Ann-first step followed by a Ben-first step—in which their first-chooser roles are reversed—yields a sequence of choices that is not strictly alternating: Ann-Ben followed by Ben-Ann yields

Ann-Ben-Ben-Ann.

This four-item sequence is called *taking turns taking turns*. To keep the terminology from getting out of hand, it is best to think of "taking turns" as *one turn* (Ann-Ben), and "taking turns taking turns" as *two turns* (Ann-Ben-Ben-Ann).

THREE TURNS, FOUR TURNS, AND MORE

Two turns need not be the end of the story. Let's suppose that, given four items, two turns—Ann-Ben-Ben-Ann—is more likely to favor Ann than Ben. We are not saying that it *always* favors Ann, just that it tends to favor Ann more than Ben.

This supposition will be true, for example, if the parties (1) rank the items the same way (for example, because of the query step) and choose sincerely (which is always optimal if their rankings are the same) and (2) think there is a bigger difference between their two most-preferred items than between their two least-preferred items.

As an illustration, suppose the four items to be divided are

- A used car (worth $3,000);
- A piano (worth $2,000);
- A painting (worth $1,000); and
- A sofa (worth $500).

If Ann and Ben are concerned only with the monetary value of these items, then the supposition made in the last paragraph holds: The difference in value between the car and the piano ($1,000) is greater than the difference in value between the painting and the sofa ($500).

Thus, it is true in this case that Ann will be favored by two turns. By first choosing the car, after which Ben chooses the piano and painting, after which Ann chooses the sofa, Ann ends up with $3,500 worth of goods compared to Ben's $3,000 worth of goods.

If, as we argued, Ann tends to be favored by two turns, is the repetition of this sequence for eight items really fair? Putting together two of the "Ann-Ben-Ben-Ann" sequences, we have Ann-Ben-Ben-Ann followed by Ann-Ben-Ben-Ann, which yields

Ann-Ben-Ben-Ann-Ann-Ben-Ben-Ann (*two turns repeated*).

Notice that the juxtaposition of two sequences of two turns, or two turns repeated, can also be described as follows: Ann chooses a single item first, then Ben and Ann alternate choosing two items at a time, with a single item chosen by Ann on the last turn. When this pattern is used in professional sports drafts, with the teams choosing two players at a time after the first team chooses a single player, it is called the *modified draft*. More common is the use of strict alternation for choosing players; this is called the *regular draft*.

Observe that Ann, based on our supposition, is favored by *each* of the repeated four-item sequences. Thus, it seems that she will be *doubly* favored by the eight-item sequence that results from putting them together.

To circumvent this favoritism, let's simply amend the eight-item sequence to one called *taking turns taking turns taking turns*, or *three turns*: Ann-Ben-Ben-Ann followed by Ben-Ann-Ann-Ben, which yields

Ann-Ben-Ben-Ann-Ben-Ann-Ann-Ben (*three turns*).

Notice that with the second four-item sequence, we bolster Ben's position.

We can further bolster Ben's position as the number of items increases from 2 to 4 to 8 to 16 and so on by successively adding "taking turns" to alternation. This extension is called *balanced alternation*.

Here's how it works: Assume, as before, that Ann starts, based on the toss of a coin. If there are either one or two items, we use one turn:

1 item: Ann
2 items: Ann-Ben.

If there are three or four items, we use two turns:

3 items: Ann-Ben-Ben
4 items: Ann-Ben-Ben-Ann.

If the number of items is between five and eight, we use three turns:

5 items: Ann-Ben-Ben-Ann-Ben
6 items: Ann-Ben-Ben-Ann-Ben-Ann
7 items: Ann-Ben-Ben-Ann-Ben-Ann-Ann
8 items: Ann-Ben-Ben-Ann-Ben-Ann-Ann-Ben.

For 9 through 16 items, we go to the 16-item sequence called *four turns*, arrived at by following the 8-item sequence for three turns with its "opposite": Ann-Ben-Ben-Ann-Ben-Ann-Ann-Ben followed by Ben-Ann-Ann-Ben-Ann-Ben-Ben-Ann, which yields

Ann-Ben-Ben-Ann-Ben-Ann-Ann-Ben-Ben-Ann-Ann-Ben-Ann-Ben-Ben-Ann (*four turns*).

Equivalently, this sequence for 16 items can be arrived at by replacing each "Ann" in the 8-item sequence by "Ann-Ben," and each "Ben" in the 8-item sequence by "Ben-Ann." This sequence is used if the number of items is between 9 and 16. For example, if there are 11 items to be divided, one would stop the sequence with Ann's choice of item 11.

This process can be continued for 17 to 32 items simply by substituting "Ann" and "Ben" for each other in the 16-item sequence that follows the just-given 16-item sequence (four turns). Extending the sequence from 33 to 64 items, 65 to 128 items, and so on follows in a similar fashion.

Notice that with balanced alternation, neither party ever has more than two choices in a row. This is not to say that three choices in a row is entirely unreasonable. Consider our earlier 4-item example, in which Ann got $3,500 worth of goods and Ben got $3,000 worth, based on the sequence, Ann-Ben-Ben-Ann. If the sequence were instead Ann-Ben-Ben-Ben, giving Ben three choices in a row, Ann would get the car, worth $3,000, and Ben would get everything else, worth $3,500, simply reversing the $3,000-$3,500 split of two turns. In this example, then, three choices in a row seems just as fair as two choices.

Recall that iterating from one turn to two turns is based on the supposition that, when there are 4 items, there is more likely to be a bigger difference between the parties' two most-preferred items than between their two next-most-preferred items. Thus, Ben is still behind in the sequence Ann-Ben-Ben-Ann. Iterating further by adding to this sequence Ben-Ann-Ann-Ben, which gives three turns for 8 items, helps Ben to catch up further. As more and more turns are added with more and more items to be divided, the balance is gradually set right under balanced alternation.

ADDING THE QUERY STEP

With balanced alternation now in hand, we need to reconsider the use of the query step, which was employed at the beginning of this chapter only for strict alternation. Even if alternation is not strict, it certainly makes sense to precede the choosing of items by the query step, exactly as before. This would leave only the items in the contested pile to be allocated, to which balanced alternation would then be applied.

There is, however, a question of what part of the balanced-alternation sequence to apply to the contested pile. One can start at the beginning of the sequence, or one can start at the point in the sequence that covers the items in the contested pile that remain. Because there are arguments both ways, let's look at an example—the one used to illustrate strict alternation in Chapter 2:

Rank	Ann	Ben
1	Pension	House
2	House	Investments
3	Investments	Custody
4	Custody	Pension

If we use two turns, Ann-Ben-Ben-Ann, and the players are sincere, then without the query step Ann will choose the pension, followed by Ben's choice of the house and the investments, leaving Ann with custody. Paradoxically, the supposedly disadvantaged party, Ben, ends up with his top two choices (the house and investments), and Ann with her top and bottom choices (the pension and custody).

Now let's add the query step. Ann would initially get the pension at the same time that Ben receives the house, since these top choices are uncontested. But because there is then a contest—first over the investments and then over custody (both Ann and Ben prefer the investments to custody)—these items would go in the contested pile. Now the question is whether we use (1) the sequence Ann-Ben (the beginning of the sequence Ann-Ben-Ben-Ann) or (2) the sequence Ben-Ann (the end of the sequence Ann-Ben-Ben-Ann) for the two items in the contested pile. There are arguments both ways:

1. The Ann-Ben sequence is what balanced alternation prescribes for two items if Ann goes first, and there are, after all, two items in the contested pile. This would result in both Ann and Ben's getting their first and third choices (the pension and investments for Ann, and the house and custody for Ben).

2. The Ben-Ann sequence is what is left of the four-item sequence that balanced alternation prescribes for four items. This would result in Ben's getting his top two choices (the house and

investments), and Ann's getting her top and bottom choices (the pension and custody).

Although alternative 1 seems to yield a fairer resolution in this particular example, there are certainly arguments for alternative 2. For example, notice that the outcome according to alternative 2 duplicates the outcome that balanced alternation provides without the query step. However, this is just a coincidence in the example. In general, balanced alternation (1) without the query step, (2) with it using alternative 1, and (3) with it using alternative 2 can yield three different allocations of the items.

Recall the rationale of the query step with strict alternation: It enables the parties to dispose of the uncontested items (the pension and the house in our example) before they get down to "brass tacks" and have to divide up the items that they rank exactly the same (the investments and custody). When they do so, it is a toss-up whether Ann or Ben should pick first.

Because balanced alternation has advantages in so many other ways, however, it is worth staying with here after the query step: Ann should choose first, according to alternative 1. That is, items in the contested pile should be treated *de novo*, with balanced alternation applied to them from the beginning of the choice sequence.

ASSESSMENT

Applying our three criteria for evaluating fair-division procedures to balanced alternation, the picture is brighter than that for strict alternation.

ENVY-FREENESS

Balanced alternation, by and large, does better on this criterion than strict alternation. In fact, with only item-by-item comparisons allowed, it is not difficult to show that *any* choice sequence that starts Ann-Ben-Ben must be envy-free if no two items are tied in the view of either party. But if there are exactly three items, and Ann thinks there is a tie among them, then she will envy Ben, because he gets two items to her one, or twice as much in value as she does.

EFFICIENCY

It turns out that balanced alternation and strict alternation are on a par in terms of efficiency. If only item-by-item comparisons are allowed, then whether the parties are sincere or use the bottom-up (sophisticated) strategy, the allocations under both alternating procedures are efficient.

On the other hand, if the parties can compare collections, then it is easy to find situations in which *both* Ann and Ben prefer another allocation (for example, the one resulting from Ben-Ann-Ann) to that resulting from Ann-Ben-Ben. For example, this will be true if Ben thinks two of the items are essentially worthless, and Ann thinks all three items are of approximately equal value.

Under Ann-Ben-Ben, Ann will end up with only about one-third of the total value, whereas Ben will end up with practically nothing if Ann chooses his favorite item at the start. By contrast, the sequence Ben-Ann-Ann will give Ben essentially everything that he wants and Ann about two-thirds of what she wants. Consequently, both parties do dramatically better with an allocation that is different from that provided by the balanced-alternation choice sequence assumed so far, which makes it inefficient.

EQUITABILITY

As with strict alternation, equitability is difficult to measure, based only on player rankings. Suffice it to say that balanced alternation, at least at an intuitive level, is more equitable because the second chooser has more opportunities to pick higher-ranked items under balanced alternation than he or she does under strict alternation.

EXTENSIONS TO THREE OR MORE PARTIES

BALANCED ALTERNATION

To generalize balanced alternation to three or more parties, let's start with three people, Ann, Ben, and Carol, and identify them by their initials, A, B, and C. Suppose it is determined by some random device that they will go in the order ABC. If there are 1 to 3 items, taking turns, or simply one turn, then they make their choices in the following sequence:

1 to 3 items: ABC (*one turn*).

Taking turns taking turns, or two turns, reverses the order of choice for the next 3 items: ABC followed by CBA, which yields

4 to 6 items: ABCCBA (*two turns*).

The double choice of C means that C is able, in a sense, to make up for going last initially by going first on the second turn.

We continue this process by interchanging A and C in the two-turn sequence to generate three turns: ABCCBA followed by CBAABC, which yields

7 to 12 items: ABCCBACBAABC (*three turns*).

Notice that if we delete C from the three-turn sequence, we get ABBABAAB; if we delete B, we get ACCACAAC; and if we delete A, we get BCCBCBBC. Thus, three turns with three persons and 12 items generalizes our earlier two-person, 8-item sequence.

In four-person situations, in which D is the fourth person, we have the following sequences:

1 to 4 items: ABCD (*one turn*)
5 to 8 items: ABCDDCBA (*two turns*)
9 to 16 items: ABCDDCBADCBAABCD (*three turns*).

In the three-turn sequence for four people, notice that if we select any two people—say, B and D—and delete the other two people (A and C), then the resulting sequence is

BDDBDBBD,

which is just three turns for two people. In general, deleting people in this way recovers the corresponding sequence for the remaining people.

Perhaps the easiest way to think about generalizing balanced alternation to any number of people is to start with a two-person sequence. For example, for up to 32 items, we have

ABBABAABBAABABBABAABABBAABBABAAB (*five turns*).

If there are three people, we substitute the block ABC for each AB block, and the block CBA for each BA block, to get five turns for three people (and up to 48 items). Similarly, one can carry out analogous substitutions for both more people and more items.

A ROUGH MEASURE OF FAIRNESS

With three people and only three items, one is forced to use ABC, so there is little hope that B and C will be treated as well as A is (unless for B there is a two-way tie for best, and for C a three-way tie for best). But what about six items and the choice sequence ABCCBA, or 12 items and the choice sequence ABC-CBACBAABC?

In the case of six items and the sequence ABCCBA, notice that A receives *at worst* her first (assigned a value of 1) and sixth (assigned a value of 6) choices. Averaging 1 and 6 gives 3½ as her average rank. For B, the worst he does is his second and fifth choices, so he also obtains an average rank of 3½. Finally, for C, who chooses third and fourth, we average 3 and 4 to get 3½ again, so all three people are treated equally in terms of average rank.

This average-rank measure, however, provides no guarantee of fairness. If the people are dividing many small items that they agree are of approximately equal value, then all they need to do is count the number of items each receives. At the other end of the spectrum, if one item has a value of 1 for all people, a second item has a value of ½, a third item a value of ¼, and so on, then the person who obtains the most valuable item does better than all the other people put together.

Another problem that may afflict balanced alternation occurs when different people receive, of necessity, different numbers of items. For example, assume that there are three people and ten

items to divide, so someone must receive four items when each
of the other two receives three items. If average rank is a sensible measure of value in this situation, then one could divide the
proportion of items a person receives by the average rank of each
item. A fair allocation in this case would mean that the person
receiving four items would have a lower average rank than the
two other people who receive only three items each.

There is probably no "best" index for measuring the fairness
of an allocation. It will very much depend on the nature of the
items and how they are valued by the parties. While balanced
alternation, especially if there are several parties choosing,
reduces the advantage the first chooser enjoys with strict alternation, it may not provide sufficient compensation to late
choosers if the parties put great value on the same one or two
items, leaving later choosers out in the cold, so to speak.

NO ESCAPE FROM INEFFICIENCY

The real difference when we move from two parties to three
parties is the breakdown in efficiency, under both strict and balanced alternation, if the parties are not sincere. To show that all
the parties might do worse under balanced alternation, as we saw
in the case of strict alternation in Chapter 2, let's return to our
earlier example, in which three football teams ranked six players
as follows:

Atlanta	Baltimore	Chicago
Center	Halfback	Tackle
Guard	Fullback	Fullback
Tackle	Guard	Halfback
Quarterback	Center	Quarterback
Halfback	Quarterback	Center
Fullback	Tackle	Guard

Rankings

To determine the sophisticated choices, we must examine several cases (see "Determination of Sophisticated Choices," below).
These sophisticated choices are shown for two rounds of selec-

tion, wherein Chicago makes two consecutive choices during the first round (the sequence is ABCCBA):

Atlanta	Baltimore	Chicago
Center	Halfback	Tackle
Guard	Fullback	Fullback
Tackle	Guard	Halfback
Quarterback	Center	Quarterback
Halfback	Quarterback	Center
Fullback	Tackle	Guard

Sophisticated Choices

The sophisticated outcome under balanced alternation, it turns out, is the same as the sophisticated outcome under strict alternation. Thus, it is worse for all teams than the sincere allocation found for strict alternation in Chapter 2, as the following summary shows:

- Atlanta gets the center and the guard when it is sincere, which is better than the center and the tackle when it is sophisticated;
- Baltimore gets the halfback and the fullback when it is sincere, which is better than the halfback and the guard when it is sophisticated;
- Chicago gets the tackle and the quarterback when it is sincere, which is better than the fullback and the quarterback when it is sophisticated.

When each team follows its individually optimal strategy, therefore, the resulting sophisticated outcome hurts everybody, compared with the sincere outcome *under strict alternation.*

Curiously, *under balanced alternation,* the sincere outcome—compared with the sophisticated one—does not help all the teams:

- Atlanta does worse with the sincere outcome, receiving the center and the quarterback;
- Baltimore does the same with the sincere outcome, receiving the halfback and the guard;
- Chicago does better with the sincere outcome, receiving the tackle and the fullback.

DETERMINATION OF SOPHISTICATED CHOICES

Assume the choice sequence is ABCCBA, where "A" is Atlanta, "B" is Baltimore, and "C" is Chicago. Clearly, Chicago can never do better than make its two consecutive choices sincerely since it has no later choices to make. Likewise, both Atlanta and Baltimore can do no better than be sincere with their second choices. Thus, it is really only Atlanta's first choice and Baltimore's first choice (after Atlanta's) that we need to consider.

Assume, for the moment, that Atlanta begins by choosing the center. Then Baltimore can guarantee itself the halfback and the guard by choosing either player first and the other player second when it is its turn to choose (because in both cases Chicago will choose the tackle and the fullback). If Baltimore were to choose the fullback initially, or anything lower on its list than the fullback, then Baltimore would do strictly worse. Hence, if Atlanta begins by choosing the center, then Baltimore will choose either the halfback or the guard, Chicago the tackle and the fullback, and Atlanta will wind up with the center and the quarterback.

A similar analysis shows that if Atlanta begins by choosing the guard, then the best that Baltimore can do is to choose either the halfback or the center, getting both players regardless of which one it picks first. This will result in Atlanta's receiving the guard and the quarterback.

On the other hand, if Atlanta begins by choosing the tackle, Atlanta does better than it would do in both the previous scenarios. This is because Baltimore's uniquely best choice next is to choose the halfback, resulting in the following allocations:

- Atlanta gets the center and tackle;
- Baltimore gets the halfback and guard;
- Chicago gets the fullback and quarterback.

It is easy to check that Atlanta will definitely do worse if it dips below the tackle for its opening choice. Thus, we can now say what sophisticated play will produce: Atlanta will open with the tackle, Baltimore will follow with the halfback, and Chicago will choose the fullback and the quarterback during the first round. During the second round, Baltimore will get the guard, and Atlanta will be left with the center.

Most noteworthy, only Chicago, with its two consecutive choices, improves upon its sophisticated allocation under balanced alternation—obtaining its top two choices—whereas all three teams did better choosing sincerely rather than sophisticatedly under strict alternation. Indeed, Chicago's sincere allocation under balanced alternation is even better than its sincere allocation under strict alternation, in which it received the tackle and the quarterback (first and fourth choices). So balanced alternation definitely can help late-choosing parties, but not necessarily if all the parties are sophisticated.

RECOMMENDATIONS

If parties are to be treated equally, there is no good reason why strict alternation ever should be used when balanced alternation is available. In fact, balanced alternation has the same compelling features as strict alternation—asking little of the parties in terms of either stating their preferences or understanding the procedure's claims to fairness—but without the glaring weakness of creating envy in an item-by-item comparison.

The real question is whether some other alternating sequences, such as Ann-Ben-Ben-Ben when there are four items, are, in general, better than the balanced-alternation sequence, Ann-Ben-Ben-Ann. This question is difficult to answer in the abstract, because one can always construct a scenario in which the former sequence is fairer than the balanced sequence, Ann-Ben-Ben-Ann. For example, if there is one highly valued item, and the three others together do not match it in value in the eyes of both Ann and Ben, then it is certainly fairer to use a procedure that gives all three of the latter items, rather than just two, to one party.

The problem with the four-item choice sequence Ann-Ben-Ben-Ben is that it gives one party a more-than-one-item advantage (three items for Ben to one for Ann). This is grossly unfair in the common setting in which there are many items of roughly equal value to the parties. It is for this reason that choice sequences like Ann-Ben-Ben-Ben should be rejected—unless the parties themselves, before they divide things up, agree that it is the most appropriate one to use. In this case, one should defer to their consensus.

If proposed to the parties before they know where they fall in the choice sequence, balanced alternation would almost certainly be chosen over strict alternation. Nevertheless, even with balanced alternation, one party may envy another because it views the *collection* of items of the other party as more valuable than its own. The next procedures address this problem by helping parties equalize the values of different collections of items.

Chapter 4
DIVIDE-AND-CHOOSE

The Hebrew Bible tells the story of Abram (later to be called Abraham) and Lot, who traveled together and eventually reached a land that could not support both of them. This set off quarreling between Abram's herdsmen and Lot's. The solution that Abram proposed to Lot was startlingly simple:

> "Let there be no strife between you and me, between my herdsmen and yours, for we are kinsmen. Is not the whole land before you? Let us separate: if you go north, I will go south; and if you go south, I will go north." (Gen. 13:8–9)

This choice was acceptable to Lot, who chose the plain of Jordan, whereas Abram remained in the land of Canaan. In effect, Abram proposed how the land might be divided, and Lot chose the part he preferred.

HISTORY

What is perhaps most interesting about divide-and-choose is how it has been used over several millennia. Jumping from the time of the Bible about 5,000 years ago to ancient Greece, Hesiod mentions this method of fair division in his book *Theogony*, written about 2,700 years ago. The Greek gods Prometheus and Zeus had to divide a portion of meat. Prometheus began by placing the meat into two piles, and Zeus selected one.

Moving to more recent times, in *Memoirs of Reprieve* (1979), Primo Levi gives a poignant account of the use of divide-and-choose in the German concentration camp of Auschwitz in Poland during World War II:

> When the letter was finished, Grigo pulled out a ration of bread and handed it to me together with the knife. It was the custom, indeed the unwritten law, that in all payments based

on bread one of the contracting parties must cut the bread and the other choose, because in this way the person who cuts is induced to make the portions as equal as possible. I was surprised that Grigo already knew the rule, but then I thought that perhaps it applied also outside the Camp, in the to me unknown world from which Grigo came. I cut, and he praised me gallantly. That both half rations were the same was to his disadvantage but I had cut well, no doubt about that.

This account offers a clear insight into why divide-and-choose is considered fair: The divider can, by making the cut "as equal as possible," ensure that no matter what piece the chooser selects, the divider receives 50%.

Bread, of course, is a *homogeneous good*—it is the same throughout. Assuming that the two parties value it in the same way (the bigger a piece, the better by the same amount), the use of divide-and-choose is unexceptional: Provided the division is equal, both sides get the same amount in the end. But what if the good being divided is not homogeneous but instead *heterogeneous*, so that the two parties have different opinions about the value of its different parts?

This problem came up several years ago when it was time to divide archeological finds between Egypt and Great Britain. The objects were all different, making equal division impossible. The clever solution that the leaders of the British and Egyptian archeological expeditions decided upon was to let the British divide everything they found between two rooms in the Cairo Museum. After this was done, a representative from the Egyptian Ministry of Culture studied the objects and claimed the objects in one of the rooms, leaving the objects in the other room for the British.

What if the Egyptians had been entitled to twice as much as the British, making the proper division 2:1? Then the British could have divided the objects among three rooms, and the Egyptians could claim the contents of any two.

Strategizing under divide-and-choose depends very much on the information that the divider has about the chooser's preferences. Let's begin by exploring this and other questions before turning to extensions of divide-and-choose to three or more parties and offering some recommendations about its use.

STRATEGY

Ask a group of people which ones would like to be the divider, and which ones the chooser, under divide-and-choose. Often the group will split about evenly, with each side fervently expressing confidence in its answer. Can both sides be right? In a way, yes. It turns out that which answer is correct depends on what each side knows about the other side's preferences as well as on what motivates each side.

To illustrate this point with an example, suppose that Ann likes chocolate three times as much as she likes vanilla, but that Ben is indifferent between the two flavors. Suppose they plan to use divide-and-choose to divvy up a cake that is 75% vanilla and 25% chocolate, and that Ann is to be the divider and Ben the chooser.

If Ann knows nothing of Ben's preferences, then she must make the division 50-50 in her eyes to ensure that she will get half the value of the cake. Ben, however, may profit considerably from Ann's decision as to which halving of the cake she decides upon. For example, she may well cut the chocolate away from the vanilla, because she values the 75% vanilla portion the same as she values the 25% chocolate portion. This division allows Ben to choose the vanilla and receive what he thinks is 75% of the value of the whole cake.

On the other hand, if Ann knows that Ben is indifferent between the chocolate and vanilla, she can divide the cake so that one pile consists of slightly more than two-thirds of the vanilla. This pile will be of greater value to Ben than the other pile will be, because its value to him is slightly more than ½ (that is, ⅔ × ¾). On the other hand, the pile of less value to Ben gives Ann

- All the chocolate (½ of the total value in her eyes); and
- One-third of the vanilla (another ⅓ × ½ = ⅙ of the value in her eyes).

Thus, Ann thinks she will receive ⅔ (½ + ⅙) of the total value if Ben chooses what is, for him, the slightly larger piece (that is, slightly more than two-thirds of the vanilla).

But we must be careful here: Ben has a choice between two halves that Ann made almost equal for him. If Ben resents the fact that, by taking the slightly larger piece, he will help Ann considerably, he might prefer to spite Ann for being exploitative and select the slightly smaller piece.

This would be a small sacrifice for Ben, which he might actually prefer in order to gain the satisfaction of teaching Ann a lesson. There is nothing irrational about such a choice if Ben places more value on avenging his perceived exploitation than on sacrificing his (slightly) larger "half." Spite such as this, of course, is not uncommon in divorces and other personal conflicts, wherein emotions run high and each side knows very well the other's preferences for different things.

To illustrate further the strategic aspects of divide-and-choose, consider the real-life case of a couple who owned and operated housekeeping cottages in Maine. When the husband died, the wife sold the cottages and house and moved to Florida. Left behind were a number of items of no use to her, but of use to two of her children, Brad and Dick, who also lived in Maine. The items were as follows:

One 12-foot aluminum row boat
One 3-horsepower outboard motor
One piano in fairly good shape
One small personal computer
One hunting rifle
One box of tools
One 1953 Ford tractor with a backhoe
One relatively old pickup truck
Two mopeds (small motorized bikes)

For the sake of this illustration, let's suppose that we can get inside the heads of the two sons and determine exactly what fraction of the total value they consider each item to be worth. Basically, Brad has a background that involves business training and an interest in music, whereas Dick is a sportsman who lives in the country. Thus, Brad certainly has more interest in the piano and computer than does Dick. On the other hand, Dick is more interested in the boat, motor, backhoe, and pickup truck. These considerations lead to the following valuations (expressed in

terms of percentages of the total value) that Brad and Dick have
for the various items.

	Brad (%)	Dick (%)
One 12-foot aluminum row boat	6	14
One 3-horsepower outboard motor	6	14
One piano in fairly good shape	17	2
One small personal computer	17	1
One hunting rifle	4	4
One box of tools	6	2
One 1953 Ford tractor with a backhoe	2	21
One relatively old pickup truck	8	14
One moped (small motorized bike)	17	14
One moped (small motorized bike)	17	14
Total	100	100

If Dick is the divider and has no knowledge of Brad's preferences, then he can construct the following 50-50 division for
himself:

Package 1: boat (14%), computer (1%), tractor (21%), one moped
         (14%);
Package 2: motor (14%), piano (2%), rifle (4%), tools (2%), truck
         (14%), one moped (14%).

Brad will choose package 2, because he thinks it represents 58%
(6% +17% + 4% + 6% + 8% + 17%) of the total value.

If Brad is the divider, with no knowledge of Dick's preferences, he can construct the following 50-50 division for himself:

Package 1: boat (6%), computer (17%), tractor (2%), truck (8%),
         one moped (17%);
Package 2: motor (6%), piano (17%), rifle (4%), tools (6%), one
         moped (17%).

Dick will choose package 1, because he thinks it represents 64%
(14% +1% + 21% + 14% + 14%) of the total value.

It is, however, a very different story if the divider knows the
preferences of the chooser and wants to be exploitative (see
"Exploitative Strategies"). Whether Dick or Brad is the exploiter,

successful exploitation can get each one, as the knowledgeable divider, more than 80% for himself while still ensuring that the chooser, in selecting his preferred package, gets more than 50%. In practice, such exploitation would be difficult to engineer, in part because it might backfire if the chooser decides to be spiteful. More likely, however, the divider will have insufficient information to make such a fine-tuned calculation.

EXPLOITATIVE STRATEGIES

Brad and Dick are brothers and, although separated by 13 years, they get along fine. Each knows the other's preferences quite well. What if they wanted to take advantage of this knowledge? For example, if Dick were the divider, he could construct the following two packages (the percentages shown are Dick's):

Package 1: boat (14%), motor (14%), rifle (4%), tractor (21%), truck (14%), one moped (14%);

Package 2: piano (2%), computer (2%), tools (1%), one moped (14%).

For Dick, package 1 is worth 81% and package 2 only 19%. Nevertheless, Brad will choose package 2, because he thinks it represents 57% (17% + 17% + 6% + 17%) of the total value.

In fact, Dick could include the tools in package 1, making the package 1–package 2 division 49-51 in Brad's eyes, and 83-17 in his eyes, but this is really cutting it close in terms of risk. Brad might then choose package 1, because he benefits so little more from package 2, which would give Dick only 17% of the total value.

On the other hand, if Brad were the divider, he could construct the following two packages (the percentages shown are Brad's):

Package 1: piano (17%), computer (17%), tools (6%), truck (8%), two mopeds (34%);

Package 2: boat (6%), motor (6%), rifle (4%), tractor (2%).

For Brad, package 1 is worth 82% and package 2 only 18%. Nevertheless, Dick will choose package 2 because he thinks it represents 53% (14% +14% + 4% + 21%) of the total value.

SYMMETRICIZING DIVIDE-AND-CHOOSE

One can imagine escalating complications and ill will arising from the struggle between Brad and Dick for the role of divider.

True, the outcome will be efficient—one side cannot do better without the other side's doing worse. But is efficiency worth this price? Might not equitability and the preservation of good feelings between Brad and Dick be far more important than material gain?

There is a modification of divide-and-choose that is well suited for such a situation. It is a symmetricized version of divide-and-choose, called the *moving-finger procedure*, and it leads to a division (admittedly inefficient in most cases) that both parties think is 50-50 (and thus equitable).

Here's how it would work for Brad and Dick. The process begins with a referee (for example, the executor of a will) listing the items in some order. Of course, if one item is worth more to both parties than everything else combined, then there is no recourse but to sell such an item and replace it with the money so obtained. But this recourse will probably not be necessary in most situations.

As the executor runs his or her finger down the list—in a manner analogous to a knife's moving across a cake—either Brad or Dick can call "stop" whenever he thinks the split is approximately 50-50. If the order of items is the one given earlier for this example, it will turn out to be Brad who calls stop when the referee's finger moves just below the rifle, which is the 50-50 point for him and the 35-65 point for Dick:

> Boat
> Motor
> Piano
> Computer
> Rifle
> ──────────
> Tools
> Tractor
> Truck
> Moped
> Moped

Because Dick did not yet call stop, we know he thinks the items in the top half of the list are worth less than half of its total value. It is now up to Brad to start transferring items simultaneously from above the line to below the line, and from below the line to above the line, in such a way that he (Brad) still thinks what is above the line is essentially the same value as what is below the line.

For example, Brad might move the computer below the line, while moving one of the mopeds (which he thinks is worth the same as the computer) above the line. At this point, Dick sees the division as pretty close to 50-50 also (actually, 48-52), and he can so indicate.

The toss of a coin determines who gets which half, so each of the brothers would have good reason to ensure that the division is approximately 50-50, as he sees it, before the choice is made of which brother gets which half. Thereby they can rest assured that (1) the resolution is envy-free, because neither desires the portion the other received, and (2) there will be no hard feelings caused by Dick's knowing that Brad is more pleased with the outcome than he is, or vice versa. This resolution also protects both siblings from experiencing guilt created by their own—perhaps unintentional—exploitation of the other, making the resolution "guilt-free" as well.

While the moving-finger procedure produces an equitable division, it may be quite inefficient, especially when both parties prefer different things and can mutually benefit from receiving them. But it does produce equitability, and it prevents the kind of strategizing that prompted one correspondent to recount his rather sophisticated childhood calculation:

> I was interested in a dynamic problem related to cake-cutting: which of the available two pieces of pizza to take from an unevenly sliced pie, given the rates of how quickly my sisters were eating, how much more they had to go on their current slices, the size of the available slices, the amount of cheese on the two slices, the warmth of each slice, and so on. For example, it might be best to take a very narrow slice, since I could finish that quickly and get another slice before my sisters finished their current pieces.

If this is mere "child's play," there may be good reason to worry about the vulnerabilities of fair-division schemes when adults try to manipulate them.

ASSESSMENT

How does divide-and-choose (and the moving-finger proce-dure) stack up according to our different criteria of fairness?

ENVY-FREENESS

Each party in divide-and-choose (and in the moving-finger procedure) has a strategy that will guarantee that it will not envy the other party, rendering the procedure envy-free. Of course, if the divider attempts to exploit the chooser, then a slight miscal-culation by the chooser, leading the chooser to take the "wrong" pile, might make the divider extremely envious of the chooser. Worst yet, spite on the part of the chooser may leave both par-ties envying each other for the items that each received. On the other hand, the satisfaction gained from spiting the other party may make up for this material loss.

EFFICIENCY

Consider the well-known nursery rhyme from *Mother Goose*:

> Jack Sprat could eat no fat,
> His wife could eat no lean;
> So 'twixt them both they cleared the cloth,
> and licked the platter clean.

Here Jack gets all his preferred lean, whereas his wife gets all her preferred fat. But if Jack were dividing, and if he had no knowl-edge of his wife's preferences, he would be forced to make the division so that each part contained half the lean, which would be highly inefficient, given his and his wife's tastes.

Now assume that the divider knows the chooser's preferences. Then the divider's optimal exploitative strategy always produces an essentially efficient allocation. Suppose, for example, that a wife makes the division 49-51 in her husband's opinion and 70-30 in hers. Assuming the husband chooses the second package, getting 51% of what he wants, the wife will get the first package, getting 70% of what she wants.

Now let's suppose that some other allocation makes the wife better off without hurting her husband. Thus, for example, assume he still gets 51% in his opinion, but she gets 71% in hers. Then, speaking strategically, instead of making the previous division, the wife could keep his portion at 51% and obtain slightly more (71%) in her opinion. As long as the wife picks from among all such 49-51 divisions the one that gives her the largest portion (assuming her husband selects his preferred portion), then the resulting allocation will be efficient. Of course, as seen earlier, efficiency is generally lost with the moving-finger procedure.

EQUITABILITY

Recall that, with alternation, only item-by-item comparisons need be made. By contrast, under divide-and-choose, the parties must compare *collections* of items; either the divider or the chooser may be favored, depending on the information possessed by the parties. Thus, divide-and-choose is not, in general, equitable. While the moving-finger procedure is designed to achieve exactly this equitability, it may do so at the cost of sacrificing efficiency.

EXTENSIONS TO THREE OR MORE PARTIES

The question of how to extend divide-and-choose to three or more parties first received serious academic attention during the 1940s. Important work in this field was done by several Polish mathematicians, including Stefan Banach, Bronislaw Knaster, and Hugo Steinhaus.

To give some idea of the fruits of this work and the research that followed it, assume that three people, Ann, Ben, and Carol, must divide several items. Choose one person at random—say, Ann—and have her construct three piles that she considers to be of equal value. But now what? Can we recommend strategies to the three people that will enable each to protect himself or herself against one person's getting the lion's share?

It will not do to have each person select one of the piles. Although the three piles are equal in Ann's view, it may well be that Ben and Carol think that one of the piles is by far the most valuable (worth, for example, 70% of the total), whereas the other two are not worth nearly so much (20% and 10% each, for example), as shown below:

Pile	Ann	Ben and Carol
1	33.3%	70%
2	33.3%	20%
3	33.3%	10%

What can we do in a case like this?

Because both Ben and Carol think that the items in one pile (pile 3) are worth only 10%, then they can let Ann have this pile, which she thinks is worth 33.3%. Now Ben and Carol can make one large pile out of the remaining 90% (piles 1 and 2), as they view the two remaining piles, and then apply divide-and-choose to them. Thereby each of them can guarantee himself or herself at least 33.3% (in fact, 45% in this example), so all three people end up with proportional shares of at least one-third.

While this seems a good procedure for three people, it is not envy-free. Thus, for example, Ann will envy either Ben or Carol unless they happen to make the division of the remaining two-thirds, as Ann sees the other two piles, *exactly* 50-50. Barring this division, Ann will end up envying one of the two other people (but not both—it is impossible for both Ben and Carol to receive more than one-third each, in Ann's view, because she divided the items equally in the beginning, so that exactly two-thirds remains to be divided).

Envy-freeness for all three people, not just proportionality, is somewhat harder to obtain. Ann begins, as before, by dividing the items into three equal piles. Assume Ben, by the toss of a coin, is selected to go next and does not think the three piles are equal: There is a largest, a next-largest, and a smallest pile, in his opinion.

In this case, Ben removes items from the largest pile so that it ties in value with the next-largest pile. (This process of reducing the largest pile to tie in value with the next-largest one is called *trimming*.) These trimmings are set aside, and the people choose in the order Carol, Ben, Ann, subject to the proviso that Ben must take the pile he trimmed if Carol did not take it.

Carol will envy nobody, because she is choosing first and can take what she considers to be the largest pile (in terms of value). Since Ben created a tie between the two largest piles, he can take whichever of the two Carol did not take (if either), ensuring himself a pile he views as at least equal in value to the others. Finally, because of the proviso, Ann is not getting stuck with the trimmed pile. Consequently, she is also able to take a pile of at least equal value to the other piles (remember that she divided the items into piles of equal value to herself in the beginning).

The fly in the ointment is the trimmings, which Ben pared off from what he thought was the largest pile to create a tie with his next-largest pile. How can we deal with these? One answer is to repeat the same procedure on the trimmings, reducing the remaining items further. The problem is that this process may have no end, especially if we are thinking of divisible items like cake and pie, with each round producing trimmings, trimmings of the trimmings, and so on.

Practically speaking, when we are down to crumbs and then specks, the parties will not care who gets the last trimmings; the table can be swept clean without making anyone envious. In fact, however, there is another way of disposing of these leftovers— neither going on forever nor creating any envy whatsoever—that is applicable not only to three parties but also to more than three. It is called the *trimming procedure* and involves the creation of ties, like those just described. Trimming, of course, depends on the goods' being *divisible*, which means that their value is not destroyed when they are divided or trimmed.

In principle, the trimming procedure is applicable to a variety of fair-division problems involving any number of parties. These include problems with entitlements, such as might be specified by a will in estate division. As another example with entitlements, consider the allocation of ministerial positions in a coalition government. Political parties that hold more seats in parliament are presumably entitled to more prestigious ministries, such as that of prime minister or foreign minister.

The division of land into more than two pieces has been a problem throughout history, but a twentieth-century case is worth recalling, especially because it reflects an informal use of the trimming procedure. In 1943 the Allies agreed in principle to partition Germany into zones after World War II. After agreement was reached among Great Britain, the United States, and the Soviet Union, France came into the picture as a fourth party and was given part of the two-thirds of Germany that comprised the British and American zones, which necessitated one kind of trimming. But several months of technical discussions

> put the Americans and British at loggerheads. Churchill asserted a strong claim to the northwestern area, which encompassed the rich industrial resources of the Ruhr. But he had been challenged by Roosevelt, who had refused to take the southwest on the ground that this would embroil the United States in the political affairs of France. After a prolonged stalemate, FDR had finally yielded to the importuning of both State and War, for whom the issue of zonal distribution was of secondary interest.

Complicating these land-division talks, the Soviet Union created additional controversy by demanding major reparations from Germany, which Britain, especially, resisted.

Later the United States and Britain discussed exchanging the two zones they were scheduled to control, apparently because each desired the other's zone. In the end, this exchange did not occur, but the United States received transit rights through the British zone to allay U.S. fears of lack of access to the sea, which may be viewed as creating a tie. In effect, allowing access to the sea made the U.S. zone as valuable to the United States as the British zone; apparently, this concession to the Americans did not change British preferences for its zone.

Initially, the Allies were not able to reach agreement about what to do with Berlin, the largest city in Germany. Berlin was simply too valuable a "piece" for the western Allies (Britain, France, and the United States) to cede to the Soviets. Subsequently, the Allies decided to partition Berlin itself into four zones, even though this city fell 110 miles within the Soviet zone. This example demonstrates how, after a piece is trimmed off, it can be subsequently divided using the trimming procedure.

RECOMMENDATIONS

Divide-and-choose was put to good use in the 1982 Convention of the Law of the Sea, which went into effect on November 16, 1994, with 159 signatories (including the United States). It specifies that whenever a developed country wants to mine a portion of the seabed, that country must propose a division of the portion into two tracts. An international mining company called the Enterprise, funded by the developed countries but representing the interests of the developing countries through the International Seabed Authority, plays the role of the other party, choosing the tract it prefers. The developed country receives the remaining tract. In this manner, parts of the seabed are preserved for commercial development by the developing countries, which—in the absence of Enterprise—could not otherwise afford to mine the seabed. Mining, however, probably will not begin in earnest for another decade, so the procedure has yet to be tested.

Clearly, when there is only one good to be divided, like an undersea oil tract or land, balanced alternation makes little sense. When there is more than one good but not too many, divide-and-choose still might be used since the combinatorial possibilities of placing the goods in different piles are not too great.

In situations in which either balanced alternation or divide-and-choose can be used, there are some definite advantages to divide-and-choose. For example, divide-and-choose provides each party with a strategy that guarantees that an allocation will be envy-free, whereas balanced alternation does not. In addition, divide-and-choose has a symmetric version that can guarantee equitability. Why, then, is this procedure so seldom used today?

The answer lies in its complexity. Balanced alternation requires only item-by-item comparisons. Divide-and-choose, on the other hand, requires that one compare entire collections, which can be arduous. Take, for example, the problem of dividing up marital property in a divorce. Robert A. Heinlein, in his novel *To Sail Beyond the Sunset: The Life and Loves of Maureen Johnson (Being the Memoirs of a Somewhat Irregular Lady)* (1987), indicates the potentially fatal consequences of using divide-and-choose:

> "Yes, dear, you have been trying to cheat me from the moment this matter of a divorce and property settlement came up." I smiled at him. "But I shan't let you; you would regret it later. Now take those two lists and rearrange them. Make the divisions so meticulously fair that you really do not care which list I take, which list I leave to you. Or, if you prefer it, I will make the division and you can take your choice. But you are not going to put all the goodies into one list and then claim that the list with the goodies is yours. So—Do I make the lists and you choose? Or do you make the lists and I choose?"
>
> It took him a week to do it, and the poor man almost died of frustration. But at least he produced new lists.

Constructing two "lists" will not always be so demanding as Heinlein portrays it to be in this divorce. Nevertheless, it will often be extremely burdensome. Worse yet, divide-and-choose may fail miserably at finding an efficient outcome in which neither party can do better without the other's doing worse.

The drawbacks of divide-and-choose also extend to strategic matters. For example, even if the divider can exploit his or her knowledge of the chooser's preferences and construct a package that this person is likely to choose—and which the divider definitely does not want—there is no assurance that the chooser will go along. If the chooser does not select his or her preferred package, whether out of ignorance or out of spite, the divider may also be left with substantially less than 50%.

The fact that the divider can prevent this outcome by making the bundles equal makes divide-and-choose envy-free. But this is no great feat if both parties end up quite unhappy—knowing that there are other divisions of the items better for both—which brings us back to the lack of efficiency of divide-and-choose. Indeed, this is divide-and-choose's great failing and, consequently, it cannot be generally recommended.

On the other hand, there are certainly situations, such as in the case of land division (in the Bible and in the allocation of oil tracts), in which divide-and-choose seems eminently reasonable. For one thing, it ensures envy-freeness, which seems especially important to preserve in personal disputes. For another, it can be symmetricized, using the moving-finger procedure, to give equitability if there are a sufficient number of items to shift back and forth between the two lists.

The trimming procedure has its roots in divide-and-choose, particularly in having parties create piles of equal highest value so as to ensure that each party can get a most-valued pile. There are, nevertheless, practical problems in creating a sufficient number of ties to make everyone happy. Also, it is not always possible literally to trim items, such as a house, in dividing up physical property, though sharing and rotation sometimes ease this kind of problem. Thus, while the underlying idea of trimming is one worth keeping in mind, rarely can the procedure itself be effectively implemented without alterations. This is the price one pays for extending divide-and-choose to three or more parties.

For two parties, however, there is a procedure that ensures efficiency, as well as envy-freeness and equitability. It is, as we will see, also relatively easy to apply.

Chapter 5
ADJUSTED WINNER

Let us recapitulate. The two alternating procedures, strict (Chapter 2) and balanced (Chapter 3), are simple to use, especially after the query step, which reduces the items that need to be divided to just those that are contested. Strict alternation, however, may give an enormous advantage to the first chooser. While balanced alternation mitigates this advantage, it has two drawbacks:

- One party may prefer the items that the other receives, creating envy;
- Even if this is not the case, both parties may not benefit to the same degree, making the resulting allocation inequitable.

If there are only two parties, and they are sincere or use the bottom-up strategy, both alternating procedures are efficient in terms of item-by-item comparisons (and balanced alternation is envy-free as well using the item-by-item criterion).

Divide-and-choose (Chapter 4), which requires that two parties be able to compare whole collections of items, is the most demanding of the procedures considered so far. For two parties, it ensures envy-freeness, but it is not efficient if the divider possesses no information about the preferences of the chooser. If the divider does possess such information, he or she can manipulate the selection of the chooser so that the resulting allocation is efficient but inequitable. On the other hand, if the chooser possesses information about the divider's preferences and decides to be spiteful, the resulting allocation will be inefficient. We also saw that it is possible to extend the rationale of divide-and-choose to more than two parties—via trimming to create ties—but this may complicate it considerably.

Can we satisfy all three of our criteria—envy-freeness, efficiency, and equitability—at once? The answer is yes, at least for two parties. In this chapter we introduce a procedure called adjusted winner (AW) which accomplishes exactly that. We then apply this procedure to a variety of fair-division conflicts in the remainder of the book.

IDEA OF ADJUSTED WINNER

Under AW, the parties to a dispute must make more difficult choices than under balanced alternation in the sense that they must attach numerical values to each item. But the procedure produces divisions with more pervasive claims to fairness than either balanced alternation or divide-and-choose.

Like both divide-and-choose and balanced alternation, AW starts with the designation of goods or issues in a dispute. The parties then indicate how much they value obtaining the different goods, or "getting their way" on the different issues, by distributing 100 points across them. This information, which may or may not be made public, becomes the basis for making a fair division of the goods and issues later.

Point-allocation schemes have been proposed for other purposes. In the mid-1980s, political scientists Russell Leng and William Epstein proposed one scheme, and political scientist Stephen Salter another scheme, to facilitate balanced superpower arms reductions, which were bogged down at the time. Under the Leng-Epstein proposal, each superpower would distribute, for example, 1,000 points over its *adversary's* weapons; the adversary would then have to destroy weapons that would reduce these points by a specific percentage, such as 10%. Under the Salter proposal, each superpower would distribute points over its *own* weapons; the adversary would then indicate which weapons it wanted destroyed whose value was equal to the specified percentage.

In the case of goods, requiring that the parties assign points to them raises the question of whether the parties will be truthful in announcing their valuations. Likewise in the case of issues, indicating how important one considers each issue by point assignments raises the question of whether honesty is consistent with good bargaining tactics.

We encountered strategic questions of this sort earlier. In Chapter 4, for example, we saw how a party's knowledge of its adversary's preferences could be used to its advantage in divide-and-choose. Likewise for both strict alternation and balanced alternation in Chapters 2 and 3, we saw how a party might exploit knowledge of an adversary's preference ranking to improve on the sincere outcome.

In the case of the alternating procedures, however, we also saw that a bad outcome for three parties could occur if they were sophisticated. In effect, their strategizing could lead everyone into a three-person Prisoners' Dilemma.

The issue of being truthful is a general one, transcending any particular bargaining or fair-division procedure. As one theorist put it,

> Preferences are usually private information, and we cannot expect people to honestly reveal them unless it is in their interest to do so. The challenge, therefore, is to design procedures that *induce* the claimants to reveal enough information about their preferences so that an equitable and efficient solution can be implemented.

We will see that AW offers, in practice if not in theory, the players such an incentive. First, however, we turn to a description of how this procedure works.

DESCRIPTION

Let's begin by illustrating AW with a specific example. Suppose that Ann and Ben are getting divorced and must divide up the following items:

1. *Retirement account.* A six-figure retirement account has been built up from Ben's employment over several years. This is valuable to both spouses, but it is more so to Ann because Ben will have more opportunity than Ann to reestablish such a fund before reaching retirement.
2. *Home.* This is a nice but not particularly extravagant house. Because Ben must remain close to his business, it is worth more to him than to Ann.

3. *Summer cottage.* This is a year-round house that is considerably less valuable than their home. But Ann realizes that she could live there quite comfortably.
4. *Investments.* These are largely mutual funds that are of considerably less value than the retirement account.
5. *Other.* This residual category includes two cars and a reasonably expensive sailboat that sleeps four, which Ben prizes.

Based on their preferences for each item, let's assume that Ann and Ben distribute their 100 points across these five items as follows:

Item	Ann	Ben
Retirement Account	<u>50</u>	40
Home	20	<u>30</u>
Summer Cottage	<u>15</u>	10
Investments	10	10
Other	5	<u>10</u>
Total	100	100

Point Assignments by Ann and Ben

AW works by assigning, initially, the item to the person who puts more points on it (that person's points are underscored). Thus, Ben gets the home, because he placed 30 points on it compared to Ann's 20. Likewise, Ben also gets the items in the "other" category, whereas Ann gets the retirement account and the summer cottage. Leaving aside the tied item (investments), Ann has a total of 65 (50 + 15) of her points, and Ben a total of 40 (30 + 10) of his points, which completes the "winner" phase of adjusted winner.

Because Ben trails Ann in points (40 compared to 65) in this phase, initially we award the investments on which they tie to Ben, which brings him up to 50 points (40 + 10). This starts the "adjusted" phase of AW. The goal is to achieve an equitable allocation by transferring items, or fractions thereof, from Ann to Ben until their point totals are equal.

What is important here is the order in which items are transferred. This order is determined by looking at certain fractions, corresponding to the items that Ann, the initial winner, has and may have to give up. In particular, for each item Ann won initially, we look at the fraction given by the ratio of Ann's points to Ben's for that item:

$$\frac{\text{Number of points Ann (initial winner) assigned to the item}}{\text{Number of points Ben (initial loser) assigned to the item}}.$$

In our example, Ann won two items, the retirement account and the summer cottage. For the retirement account, the fraction is $^{50}/_{40} = 1.25$, and for the summer cottage the fraction is $^{15}/_{10} = 1.50$.

We start by transferring items from Ann to Ben, beginning with the item with the smallest fraction. (Henceforth we will refer to this item as the *smallest-ratio* item.) This is the retirement account, with a fraction equal to 1.25. We work up to items with larger and larger fractions (there is only one larger fraction in our example) until the point totals are equalized.

Notice, however, that if we transferred the entire retirement account from Ann to Ben, Ben would wind up with 90 (50 + 40) of his points, whereas Ann would plunge to 15 (65 - 50) of her points. Plainly, transferring this entire item carries us way too far, pushing Ben into a big lead.

We conclude, therefore, that the parties will have to share or split this item. Now our task is to find exactly what fraction of this item each party will get so that their point totals come out to be equal.

Finding this fraction can be approximated by trial and error. For example, because Ben is 15 points behind Ann after the award of the investments (65 points for Ann, 50 points for Ben), we might give him 8 more points, hoping that it would reduce Ann's points by about the same number.

Now because Ben placed 40 points on the retirement account, awarding him 8 points translates into giving him one-fifth ($^{8}/_{40}$) of the account. If Ben in fact is given one-fifth of this account, he would have a new total of 58 points (50 + 8).

But how does Ann come out now? She valued the retirement account at 50 points, so giving up one-fifth of it means reducing her point total by 10 points. Thus, Ann would receive 55 (65 - 10) of her points. Because Ben is now ahead of Ann with 58 of his points to 55 of hers, we have transferred a bit too much from Ann to Ben.

A little algebra helps us find the exact amount of the retirement account that we need to transfer from Ann to Ben in order to equalize their point totals. Let x denote the fraction of the account that Ben will get. After the transfer, Ben's point total will be $50 + 40x$, and Ann's point total will be $65 - 50x$. Because we want these point totals to be equal, we want to choose x so that it satisfies

$$50 + 40x = 65 - 50x.$$

Solving for x, we find

$$90x = 15$$
$$x = {}^{15}\!/_{90} = \frac{1}{6}.$$

Thus, Ben should get one-sixth of the retirement account and Ann should get five-sixths.

Recall that Ben got the home (30 of his points), the other items (10 of his points), and the tied item, investments (10 points for both parties), totaling 50 of his points. Ann got the retirement account (50 of her points) and the summer cottage (15 of her points), totaling 65 of her points. With the 1:5 split of the retirement account, Ben's point total becomes

$$50 + 40(\tfrac{1}{6}) \approx 50 + 6.67 = 56.67,$$

and Ann's point total becomes

$$65 - 50(\tfrac{1}{6}) \approx 65 - 8.33 = 56.67.$$

That is, both people get exactly the same number of points, based on *their own* valuations of the different items. Subjectively speaking, then, each person does as well as the other, assuming their point valuations are honest reflections of their desires for the different items.

With the foregoing example in mind, let's see how AW works in general. Each party independently allocates a total of 100 points to the items, thereby indicating the worth of each to himself or herself, by putting one or more points on each item.

If the parties then submit their point assignments to a referee or mediator, he or she assigns the items in the following manner (the computation can be done by a computer, but this is hardly necessary):

1. Party 1 temporarily wins the items on which it puts more points, and party 2 wins those on which it puts more points.
2. Tied items on which the parties put the same number of points are awarded, one-by-one in any order, to the party with the fewer points at the time at which the item is awarded.
3. If the total number of points that each party wins is the same, then they are done.
4. Assume party 1 wins more points than party 2. Then party 1 will give back items (or parts of items) to party 2 in a certain order until both parties have exactly the same number of points. This transfer is called the *equitability adjustment.*
5. The giveback starts with the item having the smallest ratio of party 1's points to party 2's points, then goes to the item with the next-smallest ratio, and so on.

This calculation can be modified to reflect different entitlements—for example, if the divorce settlement states that Ann is entitled to three-fifths and Ben is entitled to two-fifths. The calculation for this example is given in "Unequal Entitlements," below.

Let's return to the case wherein Brad and Dick were dividing backhoes and boats in Maine. Both brothers were equally entitled to the ten different items that they received from their mother. Let's assume the percentages they associated with each item, given on p. 57 in Chapter 4, are the point allocations they would actually make. Using AW, Brad would initially get the piano, computer, tools, and the two mopeds, giving him a total of 74 of his points, and Dick would get the boat, motor, tractor, and truck, giving him a total of 63 of his points.

Giving Dick, in addition, the rifle, which is the one item on which Brad and Dick put the same number of points (4 points), still leaves Dick behind Brad, 67 to 74 points. Because the smallest-ratio item on which Brad beats Dick is one of the mopeds, for which the fraction is $^{17}/_{14} \approx 1.21$, we start with the transfer of it from Brad to Dick.

UNEQUAL ENTITLEMENTS

Assume that Ann is entitled to three-fifths and Ben is entitled to two-fifths of their divorce settlement, giving a ratio of 3/2 = 1.5 for their respective shares. Because Ann is ahead initially by more than this ratio (65/40 = 13/8 = 1.625, based on her winning 65 points and Ben's winning 40 points on the nontied items), we must award some points on the tied item, investments (10 points each), to Ben. Obviously, we cannot give him all 10 points, because the resulting ratio, 65/50 = 13/10 = 1.3, would give Ann less than her entitlement ratio of 1.5 and Ben too much.

Let x denote the fraction of the investments that Ben will get. After giving this fraction to Ben, his point total will be 40 + 10x, and Ann's point total will be 65 + 10(1 - x) when we give her the complementary fraction, (1 - x), of the 10 points. Because we want these point totals to be in the ratio 3/2, we set the ratio of their point totals equal to 3/2:

$$\frac{65 + 10(1 - x)}{40 + 10x} = \frac{3}{2}$$

$$2[65 + 10(1 - x)] = 3(40 + 10x).$$

The latter equation ensures that Ann will end up with more of her points (in brackets) than Ben will of his points (in parentheses), and in exactly the intended ratio. Solving for x, we find

$$50x = 30$$
$$x = 30/50 = 3/5.$$

Thus, Ben gets three-fifths of the investments, and Ann gets two-fifths, giving Ben 6 points and Ann 4 points. Thereby Ann will receive 69 (65 + 4) of her points, and Ben will receive 46 (40 + 6) of his points, which gives them total allocations in the ratio of 69/46, or 3/2.

This allocation is equitable in an extended sense: Ann and Ben each receive 15% more than their 60% and 40% entitlements. It is also envy-free in an extended sense: Although Ben receives less than half of all his points (46), he would not envy the two-thirds of Ann's share, which represents (2/3)(54) = 36 of his points, with which it is proper to compare his share of 46 (because he is entitled to only two-thirds of what Ann is).

Let x denote the fraction of this moped that Dick will get. After the transfer, Dick's point total will be $67 + 14x$, and Brad's point total will be 74 - 17x. Setting Dick's points equal to Brad's yields

$$67 + 14x = 74 - 17x.$$

Solving for x, we find

$$31x = 7$$
$$x = \frac{7}{31} \approx .226.$$

Thus, Dick is entitled to about 23% of one of the mopeds, and Brad 77%, which would be their shares if they sell it. Alternatively, either brother could buy out the other, paying the appropriate percentage of its sales price to the other.

However Brad and Dick decide to dispose of one of the mopeds, each will receive slightly more than 70 of his points:

$$67 + (14)(.226) = 74 - (17)(.226) \approx 70.16.$$

This number is considerably more than the approximately 57 points that Ann and Ben received from dividing up the five items in their divorce settlement.

This difference is readily explained: The valuations of the items by each person in the estate example with Brad and Dick are far more divergent than the valuations of the items in the divorce example with Ann and Ben. This makes possible more of a win-win outcome in the estate case.

ASSESSMENT

AW does well on all the criteria.

ENVY-FREENESS

It is not obvious that AW satisfies this property, but in fact it does always hold: Each party receives at least 50 of its own points and, hence, one party will not envy the other party because it will not desire to have what that other party received. Remarkably, this is true even if one party has advance information on the point assignments of the other party and exploits this information optimally. While such exploitation can hurt the exploited party, as we will illustrate in the next section, it can never force the exploited party below the 50-point mark.

EFFICIENCY

Efficiency is the hallmark of AW—there is no other assignment of items that can give both parties more points. Satisfying this property is not easy to achieve, especially in the context of point-allocation procedures. Because no other allocation can give Ann more of her points without simultaneously giving Ben fewer of his, and vice versa, AW ensures that there are no win-win opportunities being missed in the final allocation.

Decision analysts Ralph Keeney and Howard Raiffa, in the absence of a procedure for ensuring an efficient settlement, propose that the parties to a dispute first work out an "acceptable" settlement, though they leave vague what this means. They suggest that a third party ("contract embellisher") might then make adjustments in the original settlement that moves it toward efficiency—again without saying exactly how—in what Raiffa calls a "post-settlement settlement."

By contrast, AW guarantees efficiency *on its own,* assuming that the parties are honest in their assignments of points to items. In theory, the parties can benefit by misrepresenting their preferences, as we will see. Because such misrepresentation can undermine AW's attractive properties, we might worry that it will not be "safe" to buy into this procedure.

In practice, it turns out, AW is essentially nonmanipulable unless one party has advance information about the other party's *exact* point assignments. Assuming that this is not the case, a mediator can play an important but unorthodox role, especially when what is being determined is not who gets what goods, as in a divorce, but rather who prevails on what issues in a dispute (more on this in Chapters 6, 7, and 8). Thus, instead of trying to coax the parties into a compromise, which may be very difficult, the mediator can help them (1) identify the issues in a dispute, (2) agree on what winning and losing on each means, and (3) assign points to each issue based on its relative importance to the parties.

While mediators, unlike arbitrators, cannot dictate a settlement, with AW they can be more than just neutral third parties, advising the disputants on how best to reconcile their differences. Their newfound contribution stems from the fact that AW provides them with an important tool to induce the disputants to make *their own* decisions about what they most value. Thereby it encourages the disputants to reveal their interests—not just their bargaining positions—and accept responsibility for the consequences of their choices, which, after all, they effectively make by assigning points to the items in the dispute.

EQUITABILITY

This property is guaranteed by the equitability adjustment (illustrated earlier) and, hence, is built into AW by design. It says that if Ann receives 67 of her points, then Ben necessarily will receive 67 of his points. Assuming that the parties are honest in their point assignments, both will know this and, consequently, think that they came out exactly the same. By getting two-thirds of what they wanted in such a case, they both should feel equally satisfied.

Equitability is the least studied of our three properties and, undoubtedly, the hardest to assess because of its subjective nature. Nonetheless, AW satisfies this property, as well as the properties of efficiency and envy-freeness, and is the only one of our procedures that does so.

STRATEGY

Under AW, points are assigned by the parties independently, which is easy to ensure by having the parties submit their assignments separately and at the same time. But how do we know whether each party's assignment mirrors its true valuation of the items being divided?

There certainly are situations, such as one finds in divorce proceedings, in which each person will have more than an inkling of the preferences of the other person. Indeed, the intimate knowledge that a divorcing couple will have of each other's cares and concerns will frequently enable each to make rather accurate estimates of the points that the other spouse is likely to assign to the items in a divorce.

Thus, as with earlier procedures, we are led to ask whether the parties under AW can capitalize on their knowledge of each other's preferences. It turns out that if this knowledge is possessed by only one side—a relatively unlikely scenario—then the knowledgeable side can, in fact, capitalize on its informational advantage. However, if knowledge is roughly symmetric, then attempts by both sides to be strategic can lead to disaster, even without their being spiteful.

To illustrate the potential vulnerability of AW to manipulation, let's start with a simple example. Suppose there are just two paintings, a Matisse and a Picasso, and Ann thinks the Matisse is three times as valuable as the Picasso, whereas Ben sees them in just the opposite way. Thus, if Ann and Ben are sincere, their point assignments will be as follows:

Item	Ann	Ben
Matisse	75	25
Picasso	25	75

Because of the symmetry in this example, the initial assignments, in which Ann gets the Matisse and Ben gets the Picasso, require no equitability adjustment: Both parties end up with 75 points, or three-fourths of the total value in their eyes.

But now suppose that Ann knows Ben's preferences, but Ben does not know Ann's. In addition, suppose that, in the absence of better information, Ben will be sincere by announcing 25 points for the Matisse and 75 points for the Picasso, and Ann knows this. Can Ann benefit from being insincere?

The answer is yes. Ann should pretend that she likes the Matisse only slightly more than Ben likes the Matisse (he put 25 points on this item). This way, Ann will get all of the Matisse initially, as she did before, but it will appear that she is getting only a little more than one-fourth of the total value in her opinion, whereas Ben is getting three-fourths in his opinion (since he put

75 points on the Picasso). Consequently, a big equitability adjustment will be required to transfer much of the value of the Picasso from Ben to Ann.

To be more precise, let's work from the numbers in this example to see the extent to which Ann can manipulate AW to her advantage. Knowing that Ben will place 25 points on the Matisse, Ann should place 26 points on this item and her remaining 74 points on the Picasso. Hence, the announced point totals, assuming Ben is sincere and Ann is not, will be as follows:

Item	Ann	Ben
Matisse	26	25
Picasso	74	75

Initially, Ann will get the Matisse, receiving 26 of her announced (and insincere) points, and Ben will get the Picasso, receiving 75 of his announced (and sincere) points. But now, since Ben appears to have almost three times as many points as Ann does (75 to 26), there must be a large transfer from Ben to Ann.

The exact amount can be determined by letting x be the fraction of the *apparent* value of the Picasso that Ann will get. After the transfer, Ann's point total will be $26 + 74x$, and Ben's point total will be $75 - 75x$. Because we want these point totals to be equal, we want to choose x so that it satisfies the following equation:

$$26 + 74x = 75 - 75x.$$

Solving for x, we find

$$149x = 49,$$
$$x = {}^{49}\!/_{149} \approx .33.$$

This gives Ben, in particular,

$$75 - 75(.33) \approx 75 - 25 = 50$$

of his points. In fact, it will appear that Ann, also, is getting the same low number of points, which is not surprising because their announced point allocations are practically identical.

In terms of Ann's *true* preferences, however, the situation is very different. She is getting 75 points from winning all of the

Matisse; in addition, she is getting 33% of the Picasso that she values at 25 points, which might mean that Ben would have to pay Ann one-third of the assessed value of the Picasso to keep it entirely for himself. Altogether, then, Ann is getting

$$75 + (.33)(25) \approx 75 + 8.33 = 83.33$$

of her points, or about five-sixths of the total value in her eyes rather than the three-fourths she would get if she were honest. Of course, Ben could exploit Ann in the same manner if it were he, rather than Ann, who had one-sided information and capitalized on his knowledge of her preferences.

But what if *both* players know each other's preferences? Will the same kind of strategizing work? For example, what if Ann and Ben both assume that the other will be sincere? Each might then be motivated to try to take advantage of this situation, as Ann did earlier, by being strategic. Their announced point allocations would then be as follows:

Item	Ann	Ben
Matisse	26	74
Picasso	74	26

Now Ann will get the Picasso and Ben will get the Matisse; there will be no equitability adjustment, since it appears that each person gets 74 of his or her points. But because Ann really thinks that the Picasso represents only 25% of the total value, and Ben really thinks the same of the Matisse, each in fact will receive only 25 points! Patently, this is a disastrous outcome: Not only is it massively inefficient, but it also leaves each person extremely envious of the other.

A lesson that Ann and Ben might take from this example is that they should not be too aggressive in misrepresenting their true preferences. Otherwise, they might succeed only in hurting themselves as well as the other party, as we have just seen.

On the other hand, some shading of their bids for their favorite items may not be harmful. For example, if both Ann and Ben decide to back down on their truthful point assignments of 75 points to their favorite items to, for example, 65 points, then the result will be the same as if they were sincere: Ann will get the Matisse for 75 of her true points, and Ben will get the Picasso for 75 of his true points. Neither gains from this deception. However, if they back down from 75 sufficiently to make it appear that Ann favors the Picasso and Ben favors the Matisse, then we are back to the disastrous situation we had before, when each person gets only 25 of his or her own points.

Manifestly, insincerity carries with it risk, in part because successful manipulation requires not only having a good idea of your opponent's preferences—and his or her sincere point assignments—but also having some idea of what his or her *announced* point allocations will be. Without knowing the likely announced allocations, each party may end up being "too clever by half"—that is, hurting itself by being overly clever.

Unquestionably, it is safer to be naive or sincere, or almost so. Sincerity provides an absolute guarantee of obtaining at least 50% of the total value in one's own eyes, and possibly much more, as we will see in later examples. This makes sincerity a *guarantee strategy* under AW: No matter what strategy an opponent chooses, sincerity guarantees an envy-free portion to the sincere party.

EXTENSIONS TO THREE OR MORE PARTIES

Our analysis of AW so far has been quite abstract. Although Chapters 6, 7, and 8 are devoted to applications of AW, it is worth noting here that decisions about how to divide things, from cake to countries, not only are ubiquitous but also often involve more than two parties.

As a case in point, consider the aftermath of World War I, when President Woodrow Wilson proclaimed in 1918 his famous Fourteen Points. Point 5 read: "Free, open-minded, and absolutely impartial adjustment of all colonial claims"—certainly a noble ideal. It was not without reason that Wilson was called an idealist.

The reality, however, was ominously different. Harold Nicolson, a well-known British diplomat of the time, wrote to his wife, Vita Sackville-West, in 1919: "Darling, it is appalling, those three ignorant and irresponsible men cutting Asia Minor to bits as if they were dividing a cake." The three men Nicolson was referring to were Wilson, Lloyd George, and Georges Clemenceau, the heads of state of the United States, Great Britain, and France, the three most significant players in the immediate postwar settlement.

The Balkans were subject to another parceling out of land some 75 years later that also involved several parties. Interestingly, this struggle was less among the great powers for control of the region and more among local parties that sought additional territory. Their conflicts were especially gruesome in the former Yugoslavia.

Roiled by long-standing ethnic and religious divisions in the early 1990s, Bosnian Muslims, Croats, and Serbs fought a bitter battle for land, and the ridding of opposition groups under their control, sometimes resorting to genocidal policies euphemistically called "ethnic cleansing." While outside parties, first under the auspices of the United Nations and later under NATO, intervened to stabilize the situation, their success in stopping the fighting occurred only in November 1995, when a peace treaty was finally signed after 250,000 people were killed and 3 million people became refugees in four years of fighting.

At root, this conflict involved at least three major local parties and various outside parties. Insofar as this conflict and others like it, such as that between Israelis and Arabs, cannot be reduced to two-person situations, we are led to ask whether AW can be extended to situations involving several parties.

When there are more than two parties, there is no procedure that will simultaneously satisfy envy-freeness, efficiency, and equitability (see "Impossibility of Satisfying Three Properties," below). However, it turns out that it is always possible to find an allocation that satisfies two of the three properties: A procedure that gives both efficiency and envy-freeness has been obtained by Dutch mathematicians J. H. Reijnierse and J. A. M. Potters; procedures (called "linear programs") that give both efficiency and equitability have been obtained by the American mathematician Stephen J. Willson; and an equal division of each item to the parties gives both equitability and envy-freeness.

IMPOSSIBILITY OF SATISFYING THREE PROPERTIES

This example was given by two Dutch mathematicians, J. H. Reijnierse and J. A. M. Potters. Call the three parties Ann, Ben, and Carol, and assume they allocate the following numbers of points to items X, Y, and Z:

Items	Ann	Ben	Carol
X	40	30	30
Y	50	40	30
Z	10	30	40

The only efficient and equitable allocation turns out to be to give X to Ann, Y to Ben, and Z to Carol. Obviously, this 40-40-40 allocation is equitable; it can also be shown to be efficient.

But it is not envy-free, because Ann will envy Ben for getting Y, which Ann considers to be worth 50 points. If we gave Y to Ann and X to Ben while still giving Z to Carol, this allocation would be efficient, but it would be neither equitable (because each player would get a different number of his or her points) nor envy-free (because Ben would envy Ann).

Of course, this three-person hypothetical example does not preclude the possibility that all three properties can be satisfied in a particular situation; it says only that it is not _always_ possible to guarantee their satisfaction when there are more than two parties. The fact that one cannot guarantee the satisfaction of efficiency, envy-freeness, and equitability, however, means that a hard choice might have to be made among them in situations with more than two parties.

It is not clear *a priori* which pair of properties constitutes the most desirable set, and hence what would be the easiest property to give up if one had to sacrifice one property. To the degree that the three major parties in the Yugoslavian conflict considered themselves equal players, equitability might be the one most worth preserving, so let this be the starting point.

Given an equitable division of the land, envy-freeness might be more important to the parties than efficiency, because envy-freeness would undercut any charges that another party got a "better deal." Thus, the 40-40-40 allocation in "Impossibility of Satisfying Three Properties," which is not envy-free, might be worse than an envy-free and equitable allocation that is inefficient.

Rather than delving further into these issues, Chapters 6, 7, and 8 focus on two-person conflicts, to which AW is immediately applicable. This is not to say that extensions of AW should not be considered if there are three or more significant parties. But if a sacrifice is called for, it is by no means obvious which of the three properties that AW satisfies should be jettisoned.

Another difficulty is that all the extensions of AW to more than two parties have very much a "black-box" flavor. Unlike AW, which is basically a giveback procedure that is easy to understand and requires only simple algebra to solve, the extensions of AW use advanced mathematical methods that are intuitively opaque.

RECOMMENDATIONS

AW satisfies the three desiderata of efficiency, envy-freeness, and equitability, provided the parties are truthful in their announced valuations of the items in a dispute. AW is also straightforward to describe, though its application to real-world disputes will require considerable skill and substantive knowledge (more on this in Chapters 6, 7, and 8). On the negative side, AW's winner-take-all feature makes it potentially vulnerable to strategic misrepresentation, should one party have information about, or be able accurately to predict, the announced point assignments of the other.

If the items being divided are not tangible property but more intangible issues, then before AW is applied, the parties should decide what each would obtain if it came out the winner on an issue. Only on the one issue on which an equitability adjustment must be made will a finer breakdown actually be necessary.

Because this breakdown will be known only after AW is applied, the division on this issue must await the application of AW. This is a situation in which a mediator could play a valuable role. He or she could tell the parties the split on this issue but not which party is the relative winner. Each party, not knowing whether it got the larger or the smaller percentage, would then be motivated to reach a fair-minded agreement. For example, if the issue were what to call a new business product, and the split was three-fourths to one-fourth, then the two disputants (for example, the manufacturing and the marketing departments) might agree that whoever gets the one-fourth share will choose the advertising firm, but the other department will select the name of the product.

One might also use divide-and-choose to implement such an agreement, especially if there are physical items to divide. Assume, as in the preceding example, that one side is entitled to a one-fourth share and the other side to a three-fourths share. If divide-and-choose is first applied to get a 50-50 division, and then to each of the two halves, a 75-25 division can be effected.

We saw how misrepresentation by both parties can backfire if each party tries to exploit its knowledge of the preferences of the other party. Honesty in announcing one's point allocations, therefore, is generally a sound policy to follow—not just for ethical reasons but for strategic ones as well.

In a bitter divorce, nevertheless, it is entirely conceivable that a husband and wife would be so resentful of each other that their highest priority would be to spite the other person, even if this means losing many of the goods they most desire. While on first blush this calculation seems irrational, it is not if the spiteful person attributes sufficiently high value to "getting even."

That is, by hurting himself or herself in order to punish the other party, the punisher may in fact derive a net benefit. On the other hand, it seems virtually impossible (absent spies) to anticipate an opponent's point assignments exactly and, consequently, to pursue this strategy optimally. Also, the fact that both parties can get themselves into big trouble trying to outguess each other should halt the most egregious attempts at manipulation.

Beyond the sphere of divorce, some of the most severe conflicts in the world today are essentially two-person conflicts, such as those between Hindus and Muslims in India and Hutus and Tutsis in Rwanda—not to mention the persistent, if now diminished, struggles between the Catholics and Protestants in Northern Ireland and blacks and whites in South Africa.

Other conflicts, such as that in former Yugoslavia (briefly discussed in the preceding section), have more than two parties. At an international level, the Israeli-Arab conflict also involves several different countries, as well as factions within some of the countries (including Israel), which makes it decidedly a multiparty dispute.

As we saw in the preceding section, if there are more than two parties, no procedure guarantees the three properties of envy-freeness, efficiency, and equitability. By contrast, AW guarantees these properties in the two-party case if both parties are truthful. This is encouraging, despite AW's theoretical, but probably not practical, vulnerability to manipulation. Hence, AW will generally be the best procedure to use in two-party disputes in which the parties care differently about different issues. These differences, in fact, facilitate trade-offs that enable each party to win on its favorite issues.

In the next three chapters, we turn to a variety of two-person conflicts to illustrate the applicability of AW. In analyzing these conflicts and their possible resolution, the practical problems of implementing AW will be discussed.

Chapter 6

ADJUSTED WINNER:
Application to Camp David

In this chapter, we apply AW to the 30-year Egyptian-Israeli dispute, which was settled by the Camp David accords of 1978. These accords were formalized by a peace treaty in 1979 that terminated one of the most enduring conflicts since World War II.

The Camp David application serves as a springboard for discussing several practical aspects of using AW, including different methods for assigning points to issues by the disputants. Some observations about the fairness of the Camp David agreement, both actual and that achieved by AW, are offered. In Chapters 7 and 8, we turn to AW's application to other disputes, one of which, like Camp David, is an international one and to whose future settlement AW might be able to contribute.

ISSUES AT CAMP DAVID

On September 17, 1978, after 18 months of negotiation and a 13-day summit meeting, President Anwar Sadat of Egypt and Prime Minister Menachem Begin of Israel signed the Camp David accords. Their final bargaining was not easy. By the third day of their summit meeting, the animosity between the two leaders had grown so great that they refused to meet with each other face-to-face, so the remaining ten days of negotiations had to be conducted through intermediaries.

Six months later, the accords provided the framework for the peace treaty that the two nations signed on March 26, 1979. This epochal agreement shattered the view of many observers that the Arab-Israeli conflict was probably irreconcilable.

A number of factors make the Camp David negotiations an excellent case for examining the potential usefulness of AW. First, there were several issues over which the Egyptians and

Israelis clashed. These issues can be considered as if they were goods to be divided fairly under AW, except to obtain a good translates into getting one's way, or winning, on an issue.

Second, most of the issues were to some degree divisible, rendering the equitability-adjustment mechanism of AW applicable to the issue that must be divided. Third, there is now considerable documentation on the positions of the two sides on each issue, based on detailed accounts of the negotiations at Camp David by several of the participants. The empirical evidence enables us to make reasonable point assignments to each issue, based on the expressed concerns of each side.

The Camp David accords need to be seen in the context of the wrenching conflict that existed between the Arab countries and Israel from the time of the latter's creation in 1948. The Arab states, including Egypt, did not recognize Israel's right to exist and continually sought to annihilate it. However, Israel was victorious in the 1948–49 war, the 1956 Sinai conflict, and the six-day war of 1967. As a result of the 1967 war, Israel conquered and laid claim to substantial portions of territory of its Arab neighbors, including the Sinai Peninsula, the West Bank, the Gaza Strip, and the Golan Heights.

In 1973, Egypt and Syria attempted to recapture the Sinai Peninsula and the Golan Heights, respectively, in the Yom Kippur War but were repelled by Israel. Henry Kissinger's shuttle diplomacy in 1973–74 helped bring about two disengagement agreements between the warring sides but no permanent resolution of their conflict.

When Jimmy Carter took office in January 1977, he deemed the amelioration, if not the resolution, of the Middle East conflict one of his top priorities. This conflict had contributed to major increases in the world price of oil; the fallout of these increases had been inflation and slowed economic growth.

From Carter's perspective, stable oil prices required an end to the turmoil in the Middle East. Furthermore, Carter believed that the prevailing disengagement was unstable; some sort of permanent settlement was necessary to prevent still another Arab-Israeli war and the potential involvement of the United States.

Thus, after assuming the presidency, Carter almost immediately began to use his office to press for peace in the Middle East.

The original U.S. plan was to involve all the major parties, including the Palestine Liberation Organization (PLO), in the negotiations. But as talks proceeded, it became clear that the most likely resolution to be reached would be between Egypt and Israel. Indeed, Sadat at one point sent the U.S. president a letter urging that "nothing be done to prevent Israel and Egypt from negotiating directly."

By the summer of 1978, it seemed to Carter that a summit meeting was necessary to bridge the remaining gap between Egypt and Israel. He invited Sadat and Begin to meet with him at Camp David.

When the Egyptian and Israeli leaders convened at Camp David, there were several major issues on which the two sides sharply disagreed. These issues can be grouped into six categories. Much of the dispute centered on different territorial claims regarding the Sinai Peninsula, the West Bank, the Gaza Strip, and Jerusalem. Each side's most pressing concerns regarding each issue were as follows:

1. *The Sinai Peninsula*. This large tract of land was conquered by Israel during the six-day war in 1967 and remained under its control after the Yom Kippur War. In many ways it was the most important issue dividing the two sides in the negotiations. For Israel, the Sinai provided a military buffer that offered considerable warning in case of a possible Egyptian attack. Israel had set up military bases in the peninsula, including three modern airbases of which it was very protective.

   Israel had also captured oil fields in the Sinai that were of significant economic value. Furthermore, Israel had established civilian settlements in the Sinai that it was loath to give up. At one point at Camp David, Begin told a member of the American negotiating team, "My right eye will fall out, my right hand will fall off before I ever agree to the dismantling of a single Jewish settlement."

   For Egypt, the Sinai was of such great importance that no agreement could be achieved that did not include Egyptian control over this territory. Almost all observers of the negotiations concur that, among all his goals, Sadat "gave primacy to a full withdrawal of Israel's forces from the Sinai." He let the United States know at the earliest stages of the negotiations that while he would allow some modifications of the pre-1967 borders, the Sinai must be returned *in toto*.

Roughly midway through the 18 months of negotiation leading up to Camp David, Sadat began focusing almost exclusively on the Sinai in his discussions with both the Israelis and the Americans. From a material perspective, both its military significance and its oil fields made the return of the Sinai imperative for the Egyptians. But perhaps more importantly, the Sinai was highly valued by Egypt for symbolic reasons. For Egypt, "the return of the whole of Sinai was a matter of honor and prestige, especially since Sinai had been the scene of Egypt's 1967 humiliation."

2. *Diplomatic recognition of Israel.* Since its creation in 1948, Israel had not been recognized as a legitimate and sovereign nation by its Arab neighbors. In fact, almost all Arab countries remained officially at war with Israel and, at least for propaganda purposes, called for its liquidation. For Israel, diplomatic recognition by Egypt, its most powerful neighbor, was an overriding goal.

But Israel wanted more than just formal recognition. Israeli leaders desired normal peaceful relations with Egypt, including the exchange of ambassadors and open borders. Such a breakthrough would help liberate Israel from its pariah status in the region.

Egypt balked at normalizing relations with Israel, in part because other Arab nations would vehemently oppose such measures. Sadat also believed that normal diplomatic relations would take a generation to develop because they would require such profound psychological adjustments.

In the actual negotiations, Sadat asserted that questions of diplomatic relations, such as the exchange of ambassadors and open borders, involved Egyptian sovereignty and therefore could not be discussed. Recognition of Israel became so contentious that it presented one of the major obstacles to the signing of both the Camp David accords in 1978 and the formal peace treaty in 1979.

3. *The West Bank and the Gaza Strip.* For most Israelis, the West Bank and the Gaza Strip were geographically and historically integral to their nation—at least more so than was the Sinai. Indeed, the Israeli negotiating team held retention of these areas to be one of its central goals. Begin, in particular, considered these territories to be part of Eretz Israel, or the land of Israel, and not occupied foreign land. As one observer put it, "Begin was as adamant in refusing to relinquish Judea and Samaria [the West Bank] as Sadat was in refusing to give up any of Sinai." By contrast, if Begin were to give up the Sinai, he was intent on getting some recognition of Israel's right to the West Bank and the Gaza Strip in return.

For Egypt, these two territories had little economic or geostrategic worth; Sadat did not focus much on them as the negotiations proceeded. However, Egypt did face pressure from other Arab countries not to abandon the Palestinian populations in these territories. Sadat told his aides that he would not leave Camp David without some commitment from the Israelis to withdraw from the West Bank and Gaza Strip. In fact, once he arrived at Camp David, Sadat informed Carter, "I will not sign a Sinai agreement before an agreement is also reached on the West Bank."

4. *Formal linkage of accords and Palestinian autonomy.* One of the major issues of the negotiations was the extent to which an Egyptian-Israeli agreement should be tied to formal, substantive progress on the issue of Palestinian autonomy. Begin held that there should be no linkage. While Egypt and Israel might agree to some framework for the resolution of the Palestinian question, Begin claimed that this must be a separate matter, not part of a treaty between the two states.

Sadat seemed to be of two minds on this issue. On the one hand, he pushed for Israeli recognition of the Palestinians' right to self-determination as part of the treaty, holding that a bilateral agreement could not be signed before an agreement on general principles concerning a Palestinian state was reached. On the other hand, he pointed out that a truly substantive agreement on this issue could not be negotiated by the Egyptians alone. However, he opposed possible deferral of this issue to an Arab delegation, which he knew could sabotage an agreement.

5. *Israeli recognition of Palestinian rights.* From the Israeli perspective, recognizing the rights of the Palestinian people was difficult because of competing sovereignty claims between the Israelis and Palestinians. When President Carter declared at a meeting with Sadat in Aswân, Egypt, that any solution to the conflict "must recognize the legitimate rights of the Palestinian people," the Israelis reacted negatively. But because this recognition was not attached to any substantive changes (see issue 4, above), it was not viewed as excessively harmful to Israeli interests. In fact, Israeli foreign minister Moshe Dayan at one point sent a letter to the American negotiating team indicating that Israel would be willing to grant equal rights to Arabs in the West Bank.

From the Egyptian perspective, some form of Israeli recognition of the rights of Palestinians was deemed necessary. Even if the formulation was vague and largely symbolic, Sadat felt strongly that he needed at least a fig leaf with which to cover himself in the eyes of the other Arab countries. Rhetorically, such a declaration would allow Egypt to claim that it had forced Israel finally to recognize the rights of the Palestinian population, an accomplishment that no other Arab state had been able to achieve. Furthermore, this formulation was appealing to Sadat because it would not require the participation of other Arab states.

6. *Jerusalem.* Control of Jerusalem had been a delicate issue since 1948. The United Nations demanded in 1949 that the city be internationalized because of competing religious and political claims. Until the Israelis captured and unified the city in 1967, it had been split between an eastern and a western section.

For Israel, Jerusalem was the capital of their nation and could not be relinquished. At Camp David, Dayan told the Americans that it would take more than a United Nations resolution to take the city away from Israel: "They would also need to rewrite the Bible, and nullify three thousand years of our faith, our hopes, our yearnings and our prayers."

As was the case with other territorial claims, Egypt faced pressure from other Arab nations to force Israeli concessions on this issue. An Egyptian representative impressed on the Israelis that a constructive plan for Jerusalem would "lessen Arab anxiety and draw the sting from Arab hostility." However, Egypt did not push strenuously on this issue and, in fact, seemed willing to leave it for the future.

How might AW have been used to resolve these issues as fairly as possible? Assuming Egypt and Israel have 100 points to allocate across the six issues, let's suppose they make the following point allocations:

Issue	Israel	Egypt
Sinai	35	<u>55</u>
Diplomatic recognition	<u>10</u>	5
West Bank/Gaza Strip	<u>20</u>	10
Linkage	<u>10</u>	5
Palestinian rights	5	<u>20</u>
Jerusalem	<u>20</u>	5
Total	100	100

Hypothetical Israeli and Egyptian Point Assignments

These hypothetical allocations, to be sure, are somewhat speculative; it is impossible to know exactly how Israeli and Egyptian delegates would have distributed their points had they used AW. However, it should be noted that while different point allocations would produce different issue resolutions, this would not alter any of the properties that AW guarantees—envy-freeness, efficiency, and equitability.

The hypothetical allocation of points is based on the preceding analysis of each side's interests in the six issues. Briefly, it reflects Egypt's overwhelming interest in the Sinai, Sadat's insistence on at least a vague statement of Israeli recognition of Palestinian rights to protect him from the wrath of other Arab nations, the Israelis' more limited interests in the Sinai, and Begin's strong views on Eretz Israel—that is, retaining the West Bank and Gaza Strip and control over Jerusalem. Notice that each side has a four-tier ranking of the issues: most important (55 points for Egypt, 35 for Israel), second-most important (20 points), third-most important (10 points), and least important (5 points).

This hypothetical allocation represents a truthful, rather than a strategic, point distribution for each side. Although in theory it is possible to benefit from deliberately misrepresenting one's valuation of the issues, as we saw in Chapter 5, in practice this would be difficult. Indeed, parties may succeed only in hurting themselves, as we showed in Chapter 5 and will revisit in the present case.

Initially under AW, Egypt and Israel each win on the issues on which they allocated more points than the other side (the underscored numbers). Thus, Egypt would be awarded issues 1 and 5, for a total of 75 of its points; Israel would be awarded issues 2, 3, 4, and 6, for a total of 60 of its points.

Since Egypt has more points than Israel, some issue or issues must be transferred, in whole or in part, from Egypt to Israel in order to achieve equitability. Because the Sinai issue (issue 1) is the smallest-ratio issue ($^{55}\!/\!_{35} \approx 1.57$ is a smaller fraction than $^{20}\!/\!_5 = 4.0$, the fraction for the Palestinian-rights issue), the former must be divided, with some of Egypt's 55 points on issue 1 transferred to Israel, which allocates 35 points to this issue, to create equitability.

Let x denote the fraction of this issue that Israel will obtain. Setting Israel's points equal to Egypt's yields

$$60 + 35x = 75 - 55x.$$

Solving for x, we find that

$$90x = 15$$
$$x = {}^{15}\!/\!_{90} = \tfrac{1}{6}.$$

As a result, Israel is given one-sixth of issue 1, plus all of issues

2, 3, 4, and 6, for a total of 65.8 of its points. Egypt wins the remaining five-sixths of issue 1, along with all of issue 5, for the same total of 65.8 of its points. This final distribution is envy-free, equitable, and efficient.

It should be noted that AW, using the hypothetical point allocations, produces an outcome that mirrors quite closely the actual agreement reached by Egypt and Israel. From Israel's perspective, it essentially won on issue 2, because Egypt granted it diplomatic recognition, including the exchange of ambassadors. Israel also got its way on issue 3, when Egypt "openly acknowledged Israel's right to claim in the future its sovereign rights over the West Bank and Gaza." Additionally, Israel won on issue 4, because there was no formal linkage between the Camp David accords—or the peace treaty later—and the question of a Palestinian state or the idea of Palestinian self-determination. And, finally, Jerusalem was not part of the eventual agreement, which can be seen as Israel's prevailing on issue 6.

Egypt prevailed on issue 5: Israel did agree to the Aswân formulation of recognizing the "legitimate rights" of Palestinians. That leaves issue 1, on which Egypt won five-sixths (83%), according to our hypothetical division.

As we saw in Chapter 5, AW requires that one good or issue be divisible in order for the equitability-adjustment mechanism to work. In fact, the Sinai issue was multifaceted and thus lent itself to division. Besides the possible territorial divisions, there were also questions about Israeli military bases and airfields, as well as Israeli civilian settlements and the positioning of Egyptian military forces.

Egypt won on most of these issues. All the Sinai was turned over, and Israel evacuated its airfields, military bases, and civilian settlements, some forcibly. However, Egypt did agree to demilitarize the Sinai, and to the stationing of U.S. forces to monitor the agreement, which represented a concession to Israel's security concerns. Viewing this concession as representing roughly one-sixth (17%) of the total issue seems to be a plausible interpretation of the outcome.

One problem that arises for this hypothetical case relates to the "separability" of issues. An issue is *separable* if a party's value of winning on that issue is independent of its winning on other issues. If issues are separable, then their points can be added, as assumed under AW: Winning on a set of two or more issues gives a value for the set equal to the sum of the points of the individual issues that the set comprises. In applying AW, a key question is whether issues can be treated independently of each other.

In the case of Camp David, it can be argued that the recognition of Palestinian rights was not independent of territorial issues. For Sadat, in particular, recognition may have been more important *because* of his failure to win Israeli concessions on the West Bank, the Gaza Strip, and Jerusalem.

Although finding reasonably separable issues—whose points can be summed—is never an easy task, skillful negotiators can mitigate this problem. This happened in negotiations over the Panama Canal treaty, which was signed and ratified by the United States and Panama in 1977, when the two sides reached a consensus on ten different issues that split them. An analysis of the point allocations made to these issues showed that lumping them together would have reduced the point totals of each side, indicating that under AW two sides can do best by carving out as many separable issues as possible.

At Camp David, it is likely that the two sides would have come up with a different set of issues than those considered here. This might have facilitated the application of AW if there had been a dozen rather than a half-dozen issues. Nevertheless, our list works tolerably well, at least to illustrate the potential of AW, with both sides obtaining nearly two-thirds of the total value in their eyes.

PRACTICAL CONSIDERATIONS

Let's examine the Camp David case more closely to anticipate several difficulties, when applying AW, that can arise in trying to (1) minimize AW's vulnerability to manipulation and spite, (2) make appropriate point assignments, (3) render issues separable, (4) optimize timing, and (5) define issues.

MINIMIZING ADJUSTED WINNER'S VULNERABILITY
TO MANIPULATION AND SPITE

A potential problem with AW is its manipulability, which was illustrated with a hypothetical example in Chapter 5. One side may try to manipulate its point distribution in an attempt to increase its "winnings." Assume, for example, that Israel, anticipating that Egypt would put an overwhelmingly number of points on the Sinai—enabling Egypt almost certainly to "win" on this issue—reduced its points on the Sinai from 35 to 20. (We will see the effects of the opposite strategy—increasing its allocation—shortly.) Also anticipating that Egypt would not put too many points on Palestinian rights, suppose that Israel increased its own points on this issue from 5 to 20 (corresponding to the amount it took away from the Sinai issue), hoping, possibly, to win on Palestinian rights.

Under this scenario, Israel initially is awarded issues 2, 3, 4, and 6, for a total of 60 of its points, the same as before. However, Egypt wins only issue 1, for a total of 55 of its points, because now there is a 20-20 tie on Palestinian rights.

Because Egypt trails in points (55 to 60) at the start, it is awarded the tied issue of Palestinian rights. However, because these 20 points would now put it ahead of Israel (75 to 60 points), there must be an equitability adjustment on this issue. By giving Egypt 12.5 points (62.5%) and Israel 7.5 points (37.5%) on this issue, each side would seem to end up with a total of 67.5 points, slightly more than the 65.8 points each side formerly received.

But this improvement for Israel is illusory, because it is based on Israel's *announced* rather than true preferences. In fact, this maneuver backfires in two ways. First, insofar as Israel's earlier hypothetical point allocation reflects its true preferences, it actually ends up with fewer points. Instead of obtaining 37.5% of 20 points on Palestinian rights (its manipulative allocation), it actually obtains 37.5% of 5 points (its true value), or 1.875 points in addition to its initial 60 points, giving it a total of 61.875 points. This number is less, not more, than the 65.8 points it obtains by being honest in its announced allocation, whereas Egypt ends up with more (67.5 points).

The second way in which Israel's manipulative strategy backfires in this scenario is perhaps more costly. When both parties announce their true preferences, Israel is awarded part of the Sinai issue according to the equitability-adjustment mechanism. However, in the manipulative scenario, because Israel reduced the number of points it put on Sinai, Egypt wins this issue outright and need not make any concessions to Israel. In such a case, it could be assumed that Egypt would not have to demilitarize the Sinai, or allow the stationing of U.S. forces to monitor the agreement.

Although AW is manipulable in theory, as we saw in Chapter 5, in practice it is probably not manipulable unless a party has precise information about how the other side will distribute its points. Only then can the manipulator optimally allocate its points to exploit its knowledge. Short of having this information, however, a manipulative strategy like that just described is dangerous. The manipulator may succeed only in hurting itself and helping the other side, the opposite of what it intended to do.

In fact, Israel would do better to increase the number of points it puts on the Sinai—say, from 35 points to 45 points—while putting 10 points rather than 20 points on Jerusalem. Now, after the equitability adjustment, Israel would win one-fourth rather than one-sixth of the Sinai issue. The problem with this maneuver is that if Egypt at the same time came down, for example, from 55 points to 40 points on the Sinai—thinking the latter figure was sufficient to ensure that it would win on this issue—Israel would win instead. Egypt would lose, which is exactly the opposite of what both parties want. Once again (see the manipulative calculation on p. 82), this is a case of being too clever for one's own good.

A party to a dispute might try to manipulate its point distribution in an attempt to deny the other side a good or issue—the spite strategy. Imagine, for example, that Egypt wanted to deny Israel diplomatic recognition, even though Egypt itself did not value this issue highly, by increasing the points it allocates to the diplomatic-recognition issue.

A strategy designed to deny something to an adversary is potentially costly for the same reason that a manipulative strategy designed to increase one's point total is: The additional points allocated to an issue out of spite have to come from another issue. Thereby the spiteful party runs the risk of losing on other issues. In this case, Egypt might risk losing part or all of the Sinai in order to deny diplomatic recognition to Israel.

To convince a party that manipulation is hazardous when information is incomplete, one might have it go through the exercise of allocating insincere points for itself and then test (via AW) the outcome of such an assignment against various point assignments that its opponent might make. This exercise, in the absence of having complete information about the other side's point distribution, should convince a party that honest allocations are generally a sound strategy. We already know from Chapter 5 that honest allocations always guarantee a party at least 50 of its points—even if the other party has advance information on its allocation and follows an optimal manipulative strategy—making the outcome envy-free but not equitable.

MAKING APPROPRIATE POINT ASSIGNMENTS

While honesty usually pays, it will not always be a simple matter to come up with point assignments that mirror one's valuations of the different issues. One way to facilitate this task is to have the parties begin by ranking the issues, from most to least important, in terms of their desire to get their way on each.

After the issues have been ranked, the parties face the problem of turning a ranking into point assignments that reflect their *intensities* of preferences for the different issues. In *The Art and Science of Negotiation* (1982), decision analyst Howard Raiffa discusses this problem in considerable detail, essentially concluding that a party must carefully weigh how much it would be willing to give up on one issue to obtain more on another. Thus, for the Israelis in our example, the West Bank/Gaza Strip and Jerusalem issues are worth twice as much (20 points each) as the diplomatic recognition and linkage issues (10 points each), which in turn are each worth twice as much as Palestinian rights (5 points).

To come up with such point assignments, one option for a party would be to begin by rating the importance of winning on its highest-ranked issue, compared with its next-highest-ranked issue, by specifying a ratio. Continuing down the list, comparing the second-highest-ranked issue with the third-highest-ranked issue, and so on, a party would indicate, in relative terms, an "importance ratio" between adjacent issues.

For example, if there were three issues, and the importance ratios were 2:1 on the first issue relative to the second, and 3:2 on the second issue relative to the third, these would translate into a 6:3:2 proportion over the three issues. Rounding to the nearest integer, the point assignments would be 55, 27, and 18, respectively, on the three issues. A more systematic method for eliciting weightings, pioneered by mathematician Thomas L. Saaty and his associates and called "analytic hierarchy processing," could also be used.

Another option for a party is to begin by assigning points intuitively to items. These assignments could be "tested" by asking whether various 50-point packages represent half the total value. To the extent that they do not, the initial point assignments for items would need to be modified. This process would continue until a party is satisfied that no further adjustments in its allocations of points to each item are necessary.

RENDERING ISSUES SEPARABLE

There is also the problem of making the issues in a dispute as separable as possible in order to render the addition of points on different issues meaningful. If winning on, say, issue 1 affects the value of winning on issue 2, then the points a party receives on issue 2 cannot simply be added to the points it receives on other issues—this depends on what happens on issue 1. In this sense, the West Bank/Gaza Strip issue was probably best treated as a single issue—even though the West Bank and the Gaza Strip are two geographically separate territories—because it would have been difficult to make decisions on one independently of the other.

By contrast, in some future possible agreement, it is reasonable to suppose that the withdrawal of a few hundred Israeli settlers from the Gaza Strip will more easily be accomplished than the withdrawal of thousands, or even tens of thousands, of Israeli settlers from the West Bank. Although the 1993 Oslo and the 1998

Wye River accords between Israel and the PLO intricately linked the withdrawal of Israeli administrative and security personnel from the West Bank and from the Gaza Strip, the withdrawal of settlers is an entirely different story. In a future agreement, it would probably behoove negotiators to treat the withdrawal of settlers from the Gaza Strip and from the West Bank as separate issues, especially because Gaza has no biblical significance for the Israelis whereas the West Bank (also known as Judea and Samaria) does.

OPTIMIZING TIMING

When is it most advantageous for disputants to use AW? According to former secretary of state Henry Kissinger, "Stalemate is the most propitious condition for settlement." Former president Jimmy Carter echoed this sentiment, saying that "parties must know they cannot win on the battlefield." Carter added that

> politicians have to see a significant difference between the costs of continuing with the status quo and the benefits of sitting down with the other side. A modest difference is not enough.

According to this view, it might be best to let the disputants try, on their own, to reach an agreement without AW. If they fail after repeated attempts, they may well become so frustrated and weary as to take seriously the adoption of a formal procedure like AW to break the impasse.

Of course, leaving the final shape of an agreement to any formal procedure is somewhat of a gamble, because one cannot predict the outcome with certainty. It becomes an acceptable risk to the degree that the disputants see AW as a procedure

- From which they can benefit equally, which equitability ensures;
- That provides a guarantee of getting at least 50 points (which is the same guarantee as provided by divide-and-choose), implying that it is envy-free;
- That is efficient, so the disputants can rest assured that there is no agreement, equitable or otherwise, that can benefit both more.

If one side thinks that it can frighten the other side into submission by threats, or that it can wear down the other side through endless haggling, then the equitability and efficiency of AW, compelling as they are, will not be properties that get it adopted. Indeed, it may take months or even years of impasse, as was the case in the negotiations leading up to Camp David, before the two sides are willing to contemplate certain compromises. Only then, perhaps with the help of a mediator, might they be willing to hammer out an agreement.

The attraction of AW is that it allows the parties to reach closure immediately, at least once they agree on what the issues are and what winning and losing mean on each one. These, of course, are no small matters, but it is probably easier to reach agreement on them—and then let AW find a settlement—than it is to strike a complex overall agreement without AW.

DEFINING ISSUES

Identifying the key issues, and rendering them as separable as possible, is likely to be time-consuming, requiring protracted negotiations before the players can implement AW. But if the costs of delay are substantial, and the issues are quite narrowly defined, then the two sides should be able to reach agreement on these issues more quickly than if they try to reach a consensus without AW.

The determination of what is entailed by winning and losing on each issue would have to be worked out beforehand. As with the definition of the issues, this determination will require good-faith negotiations, possibly aided by a mediator. Also, some way of monitoring and enforcing the agreements reached on each issue—whoever wins or loses—would have to be built into the agreement once it is implemented.

After AW is applied, the two sides will also have to decide what winning and losing in relative terms mean on the one issue on which there is an equitability adjustment. In the case of Camp David, it was suggested earlier that the demilitarization of the Sinai, and the stationing of U.S. forces to monitor the agreement, were tantamount to Israel's winning one-sixth on this issue.

Negotiations on what partially winning and partially losing mean on the equitability-adjustment issue can await the application of AW, as we saw in Chapter 5. Once the equitability adjustment is known, and on what issue, the parties can be told this information (for example, a 5:1 split on the Sinai issue is required), but not which party is the relative (five-sixths) winner and which the relative (one-sixth) loser.

At this point they would be told to negotiate two agreements, one in which Israel is the five-sixths winner and one in which Egypt is the five-sixths winner. This negotiation will be facilitated by the fact that either party could be the one-sixth loser. Thus, if one side asks for the moon—figuratively speaking—if it should be the winner, so can the other side. This will chasten both sides to be fair-minded, lest the loser, which could be either side, ends up doing very badly. Thereby both sides will be motivated to reach agreement on what being the five-sixths winner means, whichever side this turns out to be.

None of the aforementioned practical considerations presents insuperable barriers to the use of AW. In order for the procedure to work best, the two sides would have to be educated as to the risks of trying to manipulate AW to their advantage or out of spite, including the likelihood that such manipulative strategies could backfire. They would also have to be advised on how best to define issues to make them as separable as possible, thereby ensuring that the addition of points across different issues, once AW is applied, is sensible. Finally, they would have to reach agreements about what winning and losing on each issue mean.

AW does not so much eliminate negotiations as require that they be structured in a certain way, which might help the disputants avoid minutae that otherwise might entangle them and sink an agreement. Once this structuring is accomplished, AW finds a settlement that is envy-free, equitable, and efficient without further haggling.

This method of achieving closure is likely to save the two sides valuable time. Additionally, it should produce a better agreement than one reached after rancorous negotiations, which often leave both sides with a bitter taste that impedes future negotiations. Not only does AW diminish this problem, but also it offers a quick way of renegotiating agreements should priorities change due to a change, for example, in government leaders or possibly fortuitous circumstances.

FAIRNESS OF THE CAMP DAVID AGREEMENT

Was the Camp David agreement fair? We believe it was, because it mostly coincided with what AW would have produced. And an AW resolution—one that is envy-free, equitable, and efficient—is our standard of fairness.

Many Egyptians were disappointed with the results of the Camp David talks. A former foreign minister of Egypt, Ismail Fahmy, wrote,

> The treaty gives all the advantages to Israel while Egypt pays the price. As a result, peace cannot last unless the treaty undergoes radical revision.

In his book *Camp David: Peacemaking and Politics* (1986), political scientist William B. Quandt also claimed that Israel did better in the negotiations. However, our reconstruction of the negotiations using AW suggests that the settlement was probably as fair as it could be. If Fahmy were correct in his belief that an unfair peace could not last, then the last two decades of peaceful relations (albeit a "cold" peace) between Israel and Egypt is testimony to the contrary.

Reinforcing this view is the fact that the negotiators, while undoubtedly desiring to "win," realized that this was not feasible because they were not in a total-conflict situation, wherein what one side wins the other side necessarily loses. Abetted by Jimmy Carter, they were driven to seek a settlement that, because it benefited both sides more or less equally, could be considered fair.

If it is surprising that a fair agreement was reached in the Middle East, it is probably more surprising that *any* agreement was concluded. In political disputes in general, and in international disputes in particular, players often expend much time and energy on procedural matters before substantive questions are even addressed. The Egyptian-Israeli negotiations were no exception: The two sides fought vigorously over procedural issues at several points in the negotiations.

Disputants have a strong incentive to do this because procedures can be manipulated so as to bring about better or worse outcomes. By guaranteeing a resolution that is fair according to several important criteria, by comparison, AW affords disputants the opportunity to focus on substantive issues—while largely protecting them from procedural manipulation.

Another problem that plagues international disputes is the concern that one side will come out looking worse than the other, which sometimes pushes the more anxious side to abandon talks altogether rather than settle for a one-sided resolution—and then attempt to explain it back home. At Camp David, Sadat at one point expressed such a fear and packed his bags on the eleventh day with the intent of returning to Egypt. Only a strong personal appeal from Jimmy Carter, coupled with pointed threats, kept Sadat from breaking off the negotiations.

By guaranteeing an outcome with very appealing properties, AW can reduce the fears of the disputants and help keep negotiations on track. In all likelihood, it would have worked well in the Egyptian-Israeli conflict—producing a less crisis-driven atmosphere than was the case at Camp David, and possibly speeding up a settlement by two or three years—even if the outcome would not have differed much from that which actually was achieved.

This is not to say that fair-division procedures like AW are without shortcomings. For one thing, formal procedures do not have the flexibility of informal approaches, though "flexibility" can be a double-edged sword that, in finding shortcuts, produces arbitrary results. While the synergy of issues poses difficulties for rendering them separable, their adroit packaging can attenuate this problem.

The benefits of a straightforward procedure that guarantees important properties of fairness should not be underestimated. Fairness, or the lack thereof, has long been a battle cry of people who feel either disadvantaged or exploited. To the extent that AW can help relieve their distress by resolving conflicts, it offers bright promise for the future. Chapters 7 and 8 explore probable outcomes that AW would give in recent disputes, most of a very different character from the sovereignty, security, and territorial issues of Camp David.

y, making her probably the equal of Donald and rendering
, therefore, appropriate to apply to their divorce case.

is worth noting in passing that Donald's next book, *Trump:*
viving at the Top (1990), showed life not to be so rosy for
eone so rich and famous. Perhaps he anticipated his 1991
orce, not to mention the numerous setbacks in business that
ell him after the booming 1980s. In 1997, Donald decided to
arate from his second wife, Marla, in part, it seems, for finan-
reasons. He professed that he wanted to be "fair" to Marla but,
ding to their prenuptial agreement, indicated that "Hey, a deal
s a deal." Donald describes his purported recovery from dis-
er in his third book, *Trump: The Art of the Comeback* (1997).
he lawyers on both sides of the divorce from Ivana were pes-
istic that Donald and Ivana could reach a satisfactory agreement
their own. A long and costly court battle seemed inevitable,
ecially in light of the prenuptial and postnuptial agreements
de by the Trumps that were later contested by Ivana.

n the Trump's prenuptial agreement, which was revised three
es during their marriage, Ivana was entitled to a settlement of
ut $14 million and the couple's Greenwich, Connecticut,
nsion. In addition, she waived her right to marital property in
first three agreements. Her lawyers argued, however, that she
er did in the fourth agreement, which was the basis of a law-
t she initiated in early 1990.

n this lawsuit, she demanded half of all marital assets, which
e estimated to be about $5 billion, under New York State's 1980
rital Equitable Distribution Law. In late 1990, however, after
e Donald" (as he was derisively called) confirmed the pre-
iousness of his financial situation and the $5 billion figure was
n to be far off the mark, Ivana said she only wanted to be
ir" and abandoned her lawsuit.

Donald's main difficulty was that he had built his real estate
pire largely on borrowed money and junk bonds, which
ned sour in the late 1980s as the economy plummeted into
ession. Near bankruptcy, he turned to the banks that had lent
m money to stay afloat, and together they developed a rescue
n. But this plan, within a few months of its initiation, was

Chapter 7
ADJUSTED WINNER:
Individual Disputes

There are 1.2 million divorces in the United States alone every
year. Though hardly typical, two of the most celebrated divorces
in recent years were those of the Prince of Wales (Charles) and
the late Princess of Wales (Diana) in Great Britain—a case only
touched on in this chapter—and that of Donald and Ivana Trump
in the United States. The Trump divorce, which we analyze in
some detail here, mirrors the Camp David outcome in the sense
of having an AW resolution that is quite close to the settlement
that the Trumps and their lawyers actually achieved on their own.

This was also true of the dispute between the 1996 Democratic
and Republican presidential candidates about the composition
and nature of their debates. This dispute was resolved only a few
weeks before the November election; the AW result closely
matched the compromise that the advisers of Bill Clinton and
Bob Dole negotiated.

In retrospect, the settlements in both the divorce and debates
cases are not particularly surprising. When two disputants have
something to gain from a settlement, one would expect them to
realize these gains, presuming they have sufficient good will and
perseverance to see the negotiations through to a conclusion.

Unfortunately for other disputants, especially in divorce cases,
these ingredients often seem to be sorely lacking. It is in these situations that AW can fulfill its most useful role, which is not that of
just ratifying or speeding up an agreement that could have been
made without it but in bringing an otherwise interminable or costly battle to some mutually acceptable resolution. It may be one
that the disputants did not even contemplate prior to AW's use,
illustrating the creative role that AW can play in dispute resolution.

Conflicts between individuals are ubiquitous both in the workplace and at home, especially with respect to the responsibilities

and obligations of each person. At home, spouses frequently quarrel over the division of household chores, which commends AW as a fair way to determine who does what: "Winning" on a chore would mean not having to do it—the other person would—which addresses the so-called *chores problem*. At work AW could be used to assign tasks, whereby each person would bid for the tasks he or she wants to do (if they are considered goods) or does not want to do (if they are considered "bads").

Indeed, goods and bads could be combined on the same list. Thus, if two company employees agreed that the task to "contact prospective customers" was a good but "handle complaints" was a bad, then both tasks could be put on the same "goods" list if the second task were written as "don't handle complaints." Using AW to assign tasks, each employee would then have to decide whether contacting prospective customers was worth fewer or more points than not handling complaints.

DIVORCE

Two divorces made the headlines in the 1990s: that terminating the 13-year marriage of Donald and Ivana Trump in 1991, and the final break-up of the 15-year marriage of the Prince and Princess of Wales, Charles and Diana, in 1996. These divorces were anything but typical: They involved mind-boggling assets, public-relations campaigns, and marital infidelities replete with photos of the extramarital lovers splashed across the front pages of newspapers. Perhaps surprisingly, these divorces involved no dispute over the custody of the children in each marriage.

The more typical problems of fair division of goods or issues among divorcing couples, and how AW might alleviate them, are discussed later. Let's start, however, with the highly atypical problems of the royal couple.

The Prince and Princess of Wales fought over not only money and property, including jewelry and horses, but also titles. Would Diana still be entitled to be addressed as "Her Royal Highness," regarded as a member of the Royal Family, or stripped of all association with Buckingham Palace? As for Charles, how much

would he have to pay Diana to settle? Lo[...] ground was Charles's mother, Queen Elizabe[...] probably bankrolled Charles's monetary pay[...] to Diana.

Indeed, Queen Elizabeth seems to have be[...] reluctantly decided that the couple's prior se[...] formalized by divorce. The couple's children,[...] Prince Henry (ages 14 and 11 at the time of[...] not an issue, in part because they spent the be[...] in boarding school. Also, they had been alter[...] school vacations with each parent after the la[...] a few years before the divorce, which was a[...] had proved successful and was satisfactory t[...]

Diana put great weight on receiving a lump[...] Charles so as not to be dependent on him ye[...] cially if she should choose to remarry. She a[...] tinue her role as "queen of the peoples' h[...] ambassador," whereas the prince and the que[...] imize her association with the palace and for h[...] bills" (her lifestyle had been an extravagant c[...]

Both sides seem to have won, relatively[...] issues most important to them, suggesting ar[...] without the application of AW's formal appara[...] prising insofar as AW replicates, as in the C[...] ment, what disputants—if they are successful-[...] informally.

Turning to the Trumps, they were also suc[...] a settlement, which principally involved cc[...] Many couples, however, are less successful n[...] property, which often has sentimental value, [...] with the children and money.

Donald Trump's authorship of *Trump: Th[...] (1987) augured well for his finding a suitable[...] his marriage with Ivana, whom he still p[...] However, the book is less advice on working o[...] a paean to Donald's success in getting his way[...] tiations. As we will see, however, Ivana had[...]

Chapter 7
ADJUSTED WINNER:
Individual Disputes

There are 1.2 million divorces in the United States alone every year. Though hardly typical, two of the most celebrated divorces in recent years were those of the Prince of Wales (Charles) and the late Princess of Wales (Diana) in Great Britain—a case only touched on in this chapter—and that of Donald and Ivana Trump in the United States. The Trump divorce, which we analyze in some detail here, mirrors the Camp David outcome in the sense of having an AW resolution that is quite close to the settlement that the Trumps and their lawyers actually achieved on their own.

This was also true of the dispute between the 1996 Democratic and Republican presidential candidates about the composition and nature of their debates. This dispute was resolved only a few weeks before the November election; the AW result closely matched the compromise that the advisers of Bill Clinton and Bob Dole negotiated.

In retrospect, the settlements in both the divorce and debates cases are not particularly surprising. When two disputants have something to gain from a settlement, one would expect them to realize these gains, presuming they have sufficient good will and perseverance to see the negotiations through to a conclusion.

Unfortunately for other disputants, especially in divorce cases, these ingredients often seem to be sorely lacking. It is in these situations that AW can fulfill its most useful role, which is not that of just ratifying or speeding up an agreement that could have been made without it but in bringing an otherwise interminable or costly battle to some mutually acceptable resolution. It may be one that the disputants did not even contemplate prior to AW's use, illustrating the creative role that AW can play in dispute resolution.

Conflicts between individuals are ubiquitous both in the workplace and at home, especially with respect to the responsibilities and obligations of each person. At home, spouses frequently quarrel over the division of household chores, which commends AW as a fair way to determine who does what: "Winning" on a chore would mean not having to do it—the other person would—which addresses the so-called *chores problem*. At work AW could be used to assign tasks, whereby each person would bid for the tasks he or she wants to do (if they are considered goods) or does not want to do (if they are considered "bads").

Indeed, goods and bads could be combined on the same list. Thus, if two company employees agreed that the task to "contact prospective customers" was a good but "handle complaints" was a bad, then both tasks could be put on the same "goods" list if the second task were written as "don't handle complaints." Using AW to assign tasks, each employee would then have to decide whether contacting prospective customers was worth fewer or more points than not handling complaints.

DIVORCE

Two divorces made the headlines in the 1990s: that terminating the 13-year marriage of Donald and Ivana Trump in 1991, and the final break-up of the 15-year marriage of the Prince and Princess of Wales, Charles and Diana, in 1996. These divorces were anything but typical: They involved mind-boggling assets, public-relations campaigns, and marital infidelities replete with photos of the extramarital lovers splashed across the front pages of newspapers. Perhaps surprisingly, these divorces involved no dispute over the custody of the children in each marriage.

The more typical problems of fair division of goods or issues among divorcing couples, and how AW might alleviate them, are discussed later. Let's start, however, with the highly atypical problems of the royal couple.

The Prince and Princess of Wales fought over not only money and property, including jewelry and horses, but also titles. Would Diana still be entitled to be addressed as "Her Royal Highness," regarded as a member of the Royal Family, or stripped of all association with Buckingham Palace? As for Charles, how much would he have to pay Diana to settle? Looming in the background was Charles's mother, Queen Elizabeth, who, in the end, probably bankrolled Charles's monetary payment of $22 million to Diana.

Indeed, Queen Elizabeth seems to have been the person who reluctantly decided that the couple's prior separation should be formalized by divorce. The couple's children, Prince William and Prince Henry (ages 14 and 11 at the time of the divorce), were not an issue, in part because they spent the better part of the year in boarding school. Also, they had been alternating holidays and school vacations with each parent after the latter were separated a few years before the divorce, which was an arrangement that had proved successful and was satisfactory to both sides.

Diana put great weight on receiving a lump-sum payment from Charles so as not to be dependent on him year after year, especially if she should choose to remarry. She also wanted to continue her role as "queen of the peoples' hearts" and "roving ambassador," whereas the prince and the queen wanted to minimize her association with the palace and for her "to pay her own bills" (her lifestyle had been an extravagant one).

Both sides seem to have won, relatively speaking, on the issues most important to them, suggesting an AW-type solution without the application of AW's formal apparatus. This is not surprising insofar as AW replicates, as in the Camp David agreement, what disputants—if they are successful—usually negotiate informally.

Turning to the Trumps, they were also successful in reaching a settlement, which principally involved contested property. Many couples, however, are less successful not only in dividing property, which often has sentimental value, but also in dealing with the children and money.

Donald Trump's authorship of *Trump: The Art of the Deal* (1987) augured well for his finding a suitable "deal" for ending his marriage with Ivana, whom he still professed to love. However, the book is less advice on working out a deal and more a paean to Donald's success in getting his way in countless negotiations. As we will see, however, Ivana had her own cards to play, making her probably the equal of Donald and rendering AW, therefore, appropriate to apply to their divorce case.

It is worth noting in passing that Donald's next book, *Trump: Surviving at the Top* (1990), showed life not to be so rosy for someone so rich and famous. Perhaps he anticipated his 1991 divorce, not to mention the numerous setbacks in business that befell him after the booming 1980s. In 1997, Donald decided to separate from his second wife, Marla, in part, it seems, for financial reasons. He professed that he wanted to be "fair" to Marla but, alluding to their prenuptial agreement, indicated that "Hey, a deal was a deal." Donald describes his purported recovery from disaster in his third book, *Trump: The Art of the Comeback* (1997).

The lawyers on both sides of the divorce from Ivana were pessimistic that Donald and Ivana could reach a satisfactory agreement on their own. A long and costly court battle seemed inevitable, especially in light of the prenuptial and postnuptial agreements made by the Trumps that were later contested by Ivana.

In the Trump's prenuptial agreement, which was revised three times during their marriage, Ivana was entitled to a settlement of about $14 million and the couple's Greenwich, Connecticut, mansion. In addition, she waived her right to marital property in the first three agreements. Her lawyers argued, however, that she never did in the fourth agreement, which was the basis of a lawsuit she initiated in early 1990.

In this lawsuit, she demanded half of all marital assets, which she estimated to be about $5 billion, under New York State's 1980 Marital Equitable Distribution Law. In late 1990, however, after "The Donald" (as he was derisively called) confirmed the precariousness of his financial situation and the $5 billion figure was seen to be far off the mark, Ivana said she only wanted to be "fair" and abandoned her lawsuit.

Donald's main difficulty was that he had built his real estate empire largely on borrowed money and junk bonds, which turned sour in the late 1980s as the economy plummeted into recession. Near bankruptcy, he turned to the banks that had lent him money to stay afloat, and together they developed a rescue plan. But this plan, within a few months of its initiation, was declared "dead," and Donald was forced into a new agreement, which included the forfeiture of several of his properties.

Understanding Donald's serious risk of bankruptcy, Ivana realized that if she did not settle quickly, she might be no more than just another person in a long line of creditors. But Donald, not ready to strike one of his vaunted deals, saw no reason not to abide by the postnuptial agreement, which his lawyer contended was "more than ironclad, it's steel-wrapped"; Ivana's attempt to get around it would be like "trying to break down a steel door with a feather."

Nevertheless, Donald insisted that he, too, wanted to be "fair." He hoped he could reach an agreement with Ivana outside the courtroom, not incidentally avoiding all the negative publicity that would attend their struggle and put a spotlight on his financial woes.

When Ivana abandoned her lawsuit and said that she was willing to negotiate a settlement in early 1991, Donald was only too willing to comply. (It is interesting to compare Ivana's posture a year earlier: "Gimme the Plaza, the Jet and the $150 Million, Too" screamed the headline of the *New York Post* on February 13, 1990.) Disregarding the assets most likely to be taken over by the banks and the business properties to which Ivana was not entitled (including the Trump shuttle, a 282-foot yacht called the Trump Princess, and a personal Boeing 727 jet), the real estate in dispute comprised:

- A 46-room estate in Greenwich, Connecticut;
- A 118-room Mar-a-Lago mansion in Palm Beach, Florida;
- A Trump Plaza apartment in New York City;
- A 50-room Trump Tower triplex in New York City.

The couple also had to reach an agreement on a fixed sum of cash to be paid to Ivana by Donald, and child support for their three children (ages 12, 8, and 6 at the time of the divorce), over whom Ivana would retain custody and with whom Donald would have visiting rights.

Except for Ivana's estimated $1.2 million in cash and jewelry, there were no cash or receivables in the divorce; Donald was barely solvent, let alone liquid. Most of his businesses were either in the red or just breaking even. He lived off a monthly $375,000 "allowance" from one of the banks to whom he owed money.

It seems plausible that Donald and Ivana would allocate the following points to the different pieces of real estate:

Property	Donald	Ivana
Connecticut estate	10	<u>40</u>
Palm Beach mansion	<u>40</u>	20
Trump Plaza apartment	10	<u>30</u>
Trump Tower triplex	<u>40</u>	10
Total	100	100

Hypothetical Point Assignments by the Trumps

Notice that Ivana places great importance on the Connecticut estate, which had been the primary family home. Her acquisition of this property is consistent with all four marital agreements that the couple had signed.

On the other hand, Donald is far more interested in the Palm Beach mansion, which had been a vacation home. His intention was to divide its surroundings into eight large development areas, to be called the "mansions at Mar-a-Lago," while keeping the 118-room main house for himself.

Ivana has a greater interest than Donald in the apartment at the Plaza Hotel, where she was living with the children during the couple's separation. He had moved to the triplex at Trump Tower and had a correspondingly greater interest in retaining it.

Applying AW, Donald is awarded initially the Palm Beach mansion and the Trump Tower triplex, giving him 80 of his points, whereas Ivana receives the Trump Plaza apartment and the Connecticut estate, giving her 70 of her points (these initial winnings are underscored in the hypothetical point assignments). But now the equitability adjustment demands that Donald give back some of his points on the smallest-ratio item he wins, namely, the Palm Beach mansion ($^{40}/_{20} = 2$, which is less than $^{40}/_{10} = 4$ on the Trump Tower triplex).

Let x denote the fraction on the Palm Beach mansion that Ivana will get. Equalizing the points of Donald and Ivana requires that

$$70 + 20x = 80 - 40x.$$

Solving for x gives

$$60x = 10$$
$$x = \frac{1}{6} \approx .17.$$

Thus, Ivana gets about 17% of the mansion and Donald keeps about 83%. This adjustment results in each spouse's receiving 73.3 of his or her points, which is nearly three-fourths of the total value.

There is little reason to believe that the point assignments Donald and Ivana would make, had AW been used, would be other than sincere. Donald repeatedly expressed his desire for an amicable settlement, even going "a step beyond [the last post-nuptial agreement] because I happen to love Ivana." (As an aside, one might ask: "Love her more than Marla?," who was Donald's girlfriend at the time, prior to their marriage.) Because Donald probably could have successfully pursued a court case to have this agreement enforced if he had wanted to, all indications are that he looked with favor on the outcome.

Ivana, coming out of a relationship in which she had often felt dominated, wanted "nothing more than a fair and equitable share." Although she indicated a desire to "get even" early in the breakup, and later expressed this sentiment in a cameo appearance in a movie, the truth seems to be that she still loved Donald: "Many friends insist Ivana would still take Donald back. So does she. She directed one person to call me back after our interview to say she was 'still madly in love with him.' " After her breakup with Donald, Ivana remarried but got divorced shortly thereafter.

The actual settlement almost exactly matched the hypothetical AW settlement. Ivana received the Connecticut estate and the Plaza apartment, and Donald received the Trump Tower triplex. As for the Palm Beach mansion, it was not physically divided or sold, but Ivana could use it as a vacation home one month a year to be around her socialite friends, which was important to her.

In addition, Donald was obligated to pay Ivana $14 million in cash and $650,000 in annual child support, which had been stipulated in their original marital agreement. This settlement mirrors well the 17% equitability adjustment on the Palm Beach mansion.

Most divorcing couples, of course, are not swimming in the riches of Charles and Diana or of Donald and Ivana. While the latter couples undoubtedly experienced some emotional distress, it was surely lessened by their lack of concern for material necessities. By contrast, the *informal* processes most couples use in divorce lead to settlements that are, in the view of some analysts, "often contentious, adversarial, and beyond the perceived control of one or both parties."

AW could provide many divorcing couples with rapid closure of their often endless haggling over money, physical property, and the children. Like the Trumps, each spouse, because of personal circumstances or for sentimental reasons, may attach different values to different items. By indicating this with their point allocations under AW, they could both end up with what they perceive to be two-thirds to three-fourths of what they want, as did the Trumps, according to our calculation, and probably Charles and Diana as well.

If how much one item is valued depends on whether one wins another item, the items are not separable and undermine the application of AW. However, there are ways to handle this. Assume that one contested item is the house, but one spouse does not have the means to maintain it. Because winning it alone in a settlement is of little value to that spouse, the house and its maintenance are not separable.

In a case like this, possession of the house might be combined with a maintenance allowance if one spouse wins, whereas if the other spouse wins, he or she might get only the house (without a maintenance allowance). Thus, instead of treating the house as a single object in which winning means the same—possession of the house—for both spouses, it can be treated as an issue in which winning gives a different outcome for each party.

Dividing up the children of divorce is often a major problem, though joint-custody arrangements are increasingly common. If both spouses attach significant value to getting their proper "share" of them, this is likely to be the smallest-ratio item when it comes time to making an equitability adjustment.

Of course, one hopes that the issue of custody, as it was in the Trump divorce, can be resolved prior to dealing with the other issues, though this will not always be possible. If not, AW may still help a couple avoid the constant and often harmful conflict over custodial and visitation rights that is the unfortunate accompaniment of many divorces.

If there is an equitability adjustment on the children, there will typically be one party that wins more than the other. Once this breakdown is made known to the parents, but not who the relative winner and the relative loser are, one agreement will suffice: The relative winner will get primary custody, and the relative loser will have visitation rights. As we saw in Chapter 6, the two sides are more likely to reach a settlement if they do not know which side they will end up on, but in this case only one agreement need be negotiated because both parents want the same thing (primary custody).

There are three advantages to using AW in divorce settlements. First, the impersonal assignment of points will help a couple separate the strong emotions and bittersweet feelings that often accompany divorce from the actual division of the marital property, including children, that will be part of the settlement. Second, AW will induce each spouse to think carefully about what he or she most values and wants out of a settlement. Thus, the assignment of points to items will weaken one's desire to spite the other person, because to do so would be to give up points on something one may value more.

Finally, having to give up "hard" points rather than "soft" positions will minimize posturing in the negotiations prior to applying AW. For example, a wife is likely to see through a husband's threat to put a lot of points on the children or on child support if she knows he really wants to win on alimony. This threat might be effective in negotiations without AW, forcing the wife to give up alimony, for example, if she very much desires to keep custody of the children. With AW, this threat will tend to be seen as a bluff if the wife believes, in the end, that the husband will not match her points on the children.

Consider another problem that may occur when AW is used: One parent may not want a child to know that he or she is worth fewer points to that parent than the other. This problem can be solved by using a trusted referee or mediator to implement AW, who would not reveal the disputants' point allocations but simply announce the assignments. Because of the equitability adjustment, these assignments will not be a sure-fire guide to which parent allocated more points to any item.

In the end, with or without revelation of the point assignments, AW determines the final settlement. It is likely to foster compromises on the issues if, in fact, the parties are encouraged by the procedure to be truthful about what they most value.

PRESIDENTIAL DEBATES

Since 1976, live televised presidential debates have been a staple of U.S. presidential campaigns. Although the first debates between presidential nominees were held in 1960, when John F. Kennedy, the Democratic party nominee, debated Richard M. Nixon, the Republican party nominee, there was a lapse of three campaigns (1964, 1968, and 1972) before they were resumed.

In 1960, it was widely believed that Kennedy "won" in these debates. His superior performance, especially in the first of the four debates with Nixon, was regarded by many analysts as decisive in swinging this exceedingly close election in his favor. After this close call, it is not surprising that Nixon decided not to debate his Democratic opponent, Hubert H. Humphrey, in the 1968 election, which this time swung narrowly in Nixon's favor, or George McGovern in the 1972 election, which Nixon won in a landslide.

The 1996 presidential debates between Bill Clinton and Bob Dole extended the unbroken tradition of debates to six campaigns over 20 years. But the format and composition of these debates were themselves debated, as they had been in the past, before they became a reality. The four issues over which the candidates and their advisers sparred were the following:

- Inclusion or exclusion of Ross Perot, the Independence party candidate;
- Number and timing of debates;
- Length of each debate;
- Format of the debates.

Let's discuss each of these issues in turn.

1. *Inclusion/exclusion of Perot.* President Clinton, who had a large lead over Senator Dole at the beginning of the general-election campaign in September 1996, wanted Perot included, apparently believing that Perot would hurt Dole more than himself. However, the nonpartisan Commission on Presidential Debates, established in 1987 as the sponsor of the debates, recommended Perot's exclusion, arguing that Perot had no "realistic chance" of winning the presidency. (Perot in fact received 8% of the popular vote in 1996, compared with the 19% that he received in 1992 after he was included, with Clinton and George Bush, in the 1992 debates.)

Aides to the president warned that Perot might not accept the Commission's recommendation and that another sponsor, more amenable to including Perot, might be sought. John Buckley, Dole's communications director, saw this as a blatant political ploy: "The Clinton people are not cleaving to Mr. Perot out of excessive zeal for the democratic process. They are making a cold, purely political decision that his inclusion in the debates helps this president."

Dole's advisers believed that Perot would be nothing more than a distraction in the debates, and would hurt Dole's poll standings, which they desperately needed to raise. Curiously, the strength of their feeling on this issue is perhaps best conveyed by Mickey Kantor, the head of Clinton's negotiating team: "The Dole camp took the position they just wouldn't debate with him. They made it clear they would have gone with no debates rather than have Perot in."

Was this bluffing? In the view of one analyst, "Bob Dole could not afford the elimination of the debates; he would be forced to show up for a three-way debate. He is so far behind that he has few bargaining chips."

2. *Number and timing.* Clinton from the start had said that he wanted only two debates, preferably on October 6 and 13, whereas Dole desired three, the last occurring on October 20. A third debate would bring the last debate closer to election day on November 5, which would give Dole more opportunity to publicize his positions against the better-known positions of the president. Also, a third debate would give Dole more opportunity to try to whittle away at Clinton's lead as the election approached.

3. *Length.* The president, considerably younger than his challenger and already well known as an accomplished debater, wanted each debate to last two hours, reportedly believing that his opponent would not hold up as well as he would. Dole preferred a length of sixty to seventy-five minutes, in part because a third debate would make up, in total time, for the reduced length of two shorter debates.

Presumably, the preferred length of a debate is related to the number of debates and their timing, making these two issues, at least to some degree, nonseparable. One way to counter this problem would be to define a single issue that allows choices on both of the present issues at once. Thus, the single issue might be the package "two debates, two hours each," which would be the outcome if Clinton won, versus "three debates, one hour each," which would be the outcome if Dole won. But in this analysis, these issues will be kept separate.

4. *Format.* In the first debate, Clinton wished to have only a moderator, but in the second he wanted the format of a town meeting, with audience participation, a format he had shown substantial skill in managing in the 1992 debate. Dole, not as convivial as Clinton, was less comfortable with this format, although it offered him the chance to prove himself to be a "regular guy" in a more participatory setting.

The following gives hypothetical point assignments by the candidates on the four issues:

Issues	Clinton	Dole
Inclusion/exclusion of Perot	40	<u>50</u>
Number and timing	<u>20</u>	16
Length	<u>20</u>	18
Format	<u>20</u>	<u>16</u>
Total	100	100

Hypothetical Point Assignments by Clinton and Dole

The key issue for both candidates was the inclusion/exclusion of Perot, but Dole, being in the weaker position, probably felt more strongly about getting his way on it than did Clinton. Accordingly, let's assume he assigns 50 points to this issue, compared with Clinton's 40 points. As for the other three issues, it is hard to say how much more important one, rather than another, was for the candidates.

Thus, let's simply assume that each candidate gives more or less equal weight to each issue. Notice that if the candidates can make only integer (whole-number) assignments, then it is not possible for Dole to do so—after he has allotted 50 points to the first issue—because $^{50}/_3 \approx 16.67$ is not an integer. But if we assume that the issue of length is slightly more important to Dole than the other two issues, then it would be reasonable for him to assign 18 points to this issue and 16 points each to the other two.

These assignments by both candidates enable Dole, initially, to win on the exclusion of Perot (50 points for him) and Clinton, initially, to win on the other three issues (giving a total of 60 points for him). Clinton, therefore, must transfer a fraction x of points back to Dole on the smallest-ratio item (length).

Setting Dole's points equal to Clinton's yields

$$50 + 18x = 60 - 20x.$$

Solving for x gives

$$38x = 10$$
$$x = {}^5\!/_{19} \approx .26,$$

so Clinton must give about one-fourth back on the length issue. As a result, each candidate receives 54.7 of his points, a relatively small number compared with the 65.8 points that each party derived from the Camp David settlement and the 73.3 points each party derived from the Trump divorce.

This relatively poor showing of both candidates stems from their viewing the presidential-debate issues in almost "zero-sum" terms. That is, the magnitude of the win of one candidate is almost the same as the magnitude of the loss of the other candidate on each of the four issues, making them sum, more or less, to zero. Consequently, there is not much "added value" that can be derived by both candidates—what one wins, the other mostly loses—compared with the situations engendered by the more divergent positions of the disputants in the previous cases: They did not want the same things, so both sides could be satisfied more easily. Nonetheless, both candidates come out ahead, if only by a small amount, with about 55 points each.

As matters turned out, the outcome of the debate negotiations was close to what it would have been, using AW, under our postulated point assignments. Dole, whose position on Perot was certainly strengthened by the report of the Commission on Presidential Debates, managed to get Perot excluded, after which Perot vociferously attacked Dole on grounds of not only being unfair but also suppressing his legitimate right to be heard on the issues of the day. This attack might have cost Dole some Perot supporters, who otherwise would have voted for him as Perot's candidacy faded in the campaign.

Clinton won on the other issues, except for length, on which there was a compromise (the debates were 90 minutes). This compromise was not exactly according to the equitability adjustment, but such exactitude in matching the actual outcome probably cannot be achieved.

It is possible to "cook" the point assignments to do better— that is, so that they more closely approximate the actual outcome. Making perfect predictions (or, more accurately, "retrodictions," since the predictions are about how something in the past might have turned out) is not the purpose of this exercise, however;

rather, it is to ground the point assignments in the expressed preferences of the parties. Only by maintaining independence between the parties' preferences and the known outcomes of the negotiations can legitimate comparisons be made between the presumptive results of AW and the observed outcome.

Questions frequently asked in real-life cases like the ones just assayed are: Did Ivana Trump value the Connecticut estate more than the Trump Plaza apartment, where she lived (40 versus 30 points in our scenario)? Given that Bob Dole indicated he would not debate President Clinton if Ross Perot were included, would he have put "only" 50 points on this issue? These questions are vexing, even to the parties involved.

There is no magic formula for making comparisons or trade-offs. The assigning of points is certainly easier if the items in dispute are goods that one side or the other will receive, and only one of which need be split or shared.

But negotiations often involve less concrete and more inchoate items—issues—on which winning and losing are far from evident. Applying AW to issues requires first determining what these are and then deciding what winning and losing on each issue mean for the two sides, which may require arduous negotiations.

Is this effort worthwhile? The potential rewards of using AW— an efficient, envy-free, and equitable settlement—can be gleaned not only from historical cases but also from controversies that are recurrent or not yet resolved. These are illustrated in Chapter 8, in which larger organizational interests play a significant role. Indeed, conflicting corporate, national, and international interests often create logjams that individuals in personal disputes are better able to avoid.

Chapter 8
ADJUSTED WINNER:
Business and International Disputes

Labor-management disputes, including those that end in bitter strikes that can be devastating to both sides, seem prime candidates for AW. Typically, labor has different concerns from management with respect to salaries, pensions, working conditions, and the like, which can enable *both* sides to achieve a good deal of what they want.

Often outside parties are significantly affected by a labor-management dispute. One example is baseball fans, who were so enraged when the U.S. major-league teams went on a long and costly strike in 1994–95 that, even after play resumed under federal injunction, they temporarily "gave up" on the sport, resulting in diminished attendance at the baseball stadiums and lower television ratings.

Besides labor-management disputes, disagreements between businesses are common, especially when companies merge or are acquired. If each company cares more about different parts of an agreement, complex arrangements need to be worked out to satisfy both sides. These could be facilitated by AW.

One of the most elusive ingredients in the success of a merger is what deal makers euphemistically refer to as *social issues*—how power, position, and status will be allocated among the merging companies' executives. A failure to resolve these issues often leads to the destruction of shareholder wealth and the portrayal of top executives as petty corporate titans, unable to subordinate their selfish interests to the goal of promoting shareholder well-being.

In this chapter, we will see how AW could be used to reduce the likelihood of a merger's being torpedoed by social issues. That such impasse can be costly is illustrated by the aborted deal between two giant pharmaceutical companies, Glaxo Wellcome

and SmithKline Beecham, in February 1998, in which the companies "saw nearly $19 billion of their stock-market value vanish in the clash of two corporate egos."

The second illustration of AW in this chapter involves a real dispute that is unlikely to be resolved for years. This is the conflict among several Asian countries over the Spratly Islands in the South China Sea, which is narrowed down to a dispute between China and all the other claimants of these islands.

The fact that this is an ongoing dispute means that one cannot repair to an actual settlement and claim that AW could have achieved the same thing, or even a better agreement, more quickly. Rather, AW in this case serves the normative purpose of offering a way to think carefully and systematically about a dispute, if not resolve it, illustrating AW's potential as a tool for policy analysis.

MERGERS

In the aftermath of the failed Glaxo Wellcome–SmithKline Beecham deal, the financial press was full of unflattering descriptions of corporate egos run amok and the damage to shareholder interests they caused. Jan Leschly, SmithKline's chief executive, and Sir Richard Sykes, Glaxo's tough-talking chairman, were accused of suffering from the "great man" syndrome, allowing considerations of power and prestige to overshadow concerns for shareholder wealth.

The failure of these two pharmaceutical giants to resolve their differences, which would have led to the largest merger up to that time, is just one of the most recent and striking examples of merger negotiations gone awry because of the top executives' inability to agree on the division of control in the merged entity. Several months earlier, Mellon Bank Corp. and Bank of New York Co. came close to agreeing to a merger of equals, but talks collapsed over issues of management succession.

In January 1996, Boeing and McDonnel Douglas terminated their merger discussions due to their inability to agree on personnel and related issues—only to resume negotiations less than a year later because the combination did, indeed, make a great deal of strategic sense. Also in 1996, CCB Financial Corp. and United Carolina Bancshares, amid the rush of consolidations in the regional banking industry, failed to agree on a strategic merger because their executives could not resolve, among other things, who would occupy the top executive positions in the merged bank and where its headquarters would be.

The reality of contemporary deal making, in short, is that the agreement on "objective" or "quantifiable" aspects of the merger is just one of the prerequisites to the success of a deal. According to Michael Carr, co-head of M&A (mergers and acquisitions) at Salomon Smith Barney, "There are a lot of things that need to be in balance in a stock merger, from price/earnings ratios to earnings contributions to the social issues." This sentiment is echoed by Robert Kindler, an M&A partner at Cravath, Swaine & Moore: "Even transactions that make absolute economic sense don't happen unless the social issues work." *Social issues* concern the more ineffable matters of status, role, and prestige in the merged company, as opposed to "hard" financial factors.

Despite the obvious importance of social issues to the consummation of merger negotiations, merger professionals have so far been unsuccessful in developing negotiation techniques that can help corporate executives overcome their differences. The urgent need for such techniques is highlighted by the mind-boggling volume of deals recently: In just the first half of 1998, according to PR Newswire Association, Inc., the value of announced U.S. deals reached $945 billion, exceeding 1997's record full-year total of $910 billion. There were an average of 29 deals a day.

Most of the current deals are not diversifying transactions. Rather, the rationale for a typical merger is the achievement of synergistic gains by combining two companies in the same industry segment. In this environment, a company's failure to acquire or merge with another firm in order to start realizing these gains sooner than its rivals can be quite costly to its shareholders. Even if a merger is ultimately consummated, as in the case of Boeing and McDonnel Douglas, a failure to agree on the resolution of social issues quickly wastes resources and the extremely valuable time of top corporate executives.

AW can prevent diminutions in shareholder value caused by the deal makers' inability to divide social issues. In addition to providing a compelling solution to a problem that potentially can scuttle merger talks, AW can also promote harmonious working relationships between the merging companies' management teams by ensuring that each side gets what it perceives to be a "fair deal."

The latter is of crucial importance in the postmerger integration period. A recent study by Mercer Management Consulting shows that a key reason why mergers fail to live up to expectations is the inability of the merged company "to get people to work together productively."

As a case in point, a 1998 deal that may turn out to be less successful than deal makers had anticipated is the $25 billion merger between Swiss Bank Corp. (SBC) and Union Bank of Switzerland (UBS). According to the *Wall Street Journal*, a number of senior UBS executives left the firm soon after the merger because of dissatisfaction with the division of power between SBC and UBS managers.

The difficulty in forging cooperation between two management teams is perhaps inevitable, given the transformation that their relationship undergoes from the premerger to the postmerger period. After all, former adversaries, first in the marketplace and then at the negotiating table, are quite suddenly expected to work closely together and cooperate fully as their respective corporate entities attempt to meld into a single organization.

To illustrate the application of AW to mergers, suppose that two companies—company 1 and company 2—are contemplating a merger. Assume that the companies agree on an exchange ratio whereby shareholders of company 1 would own 60% and shareholders of company 2 would own 40% of the combined entity after the merger. Several social issues remain outstanding: the surviving company's name; the location of corporate headquarters; the split of the chairman and chief executive officer (CEO) positions; and, finally, which side will lay off some of its employees, particularly corporate executives, to eliminate overlapping operations or responsibilities (each company would prefer fewer of its own layoffs).

We suppose that the merging companies' executives negotiate over these issues in good faith. If, for example, one of the CEOs is clearly incapable of moving the merged company in the agreed-upon direction, or if one company has clearly superior personnel in overlapping operational areas, the issues of CEO succession or layoffs would be resolved without the help of AW. Thus, we are concerned with truly intractable issues that can be won or lost by either side without undermining the merger's objectives.

Assume that each side distributes its 100 points across the issues, as follows:

Issues	Company 1	Company 2
Name	6	<u>21</u>
Headquarters	<u>35</u>	15
Chairman	19	<u>28</u>
CEO	<u>14</u>	12
Layoffs	<u>26</u>	24
Total	100	100

Hypothetical Point Assignments by Two Companies

It is easy to show (see "Merger Example") that company 2 will decide what the name of the combined entity will be and who will be its chairman. Company 1, on the other hand, will decide where the combined entity's headquarters will be located and who will be the CEO. There will be an equitability adjustment on layoffs such that 97.6% will come from company 2 and 2.4% from company 1. This allocation gives each company 24% more than its entitlement.

Despite AW's apparent effectiveness as a dispute-resolution device, two aspects of its design may render it impractical in some merger negotiations. First, because the good or issue on which the equitability adjustment is made is not known in advance, indivisibility could be a problem. Whereas it is easy to agree on what it means that x% of layoffs would come from one side and $(100 - x)$% from the other, dividing the location of the combined entity's headquarters is hardly a feasible proposition.

Second, the procedure can, as illustrated earlier, be manipulated by a party that has inside information about the other party's point allocations across the issues.

MERGER EXAMPLE

The initital hypothetical point assignments for companies 1 and 2 (underscored) result in company 1's winning 75 of its points and company 2's winning 49 of its points, which is inequitable even with company 1's greater entitlement of 60%.

In particular, notice that $75/49 \approx 1.53$ is slightly more than the 50% greater ownership entitlement $(60/40 = 1.5)$ of company 1. Accordingly, company 1 must give back points on the smallest-ratio issue on which it won $(26/24 = 13/12 \approx 1.08$ on layoffs is less than $14/12 = 7/6 \approx 1.17$ on CEO and $35/15 = 7/3 \approx 2.33$ on headquarters).

Let x denote the fraction of the layoff issue that will be resolved in favor of company 1, with $(1 - x)$ being the complementary fraction favoring company 2. Setting company 1's points (left side of the equation) equal to 3/2, or 1.5, of company 2's points (right side), we obtain

$$35 + 14 + 26x = (3/2)[28 + 21 + 24(1 - x)].$$

Solving for x yields $x \approx .976$, so company 1 "wins" overwhelmingly on the layoff issue. Thus, 97.6% of the layoffs will come from company 2 and only 2.4% from company 1.

It is simple to verify that the allocation of social issues produced by AW is, in fact, equitable in an extended sense: company 1 wins $35 + 14 + 26(.976) \approx 74.4$ of its points, and company 2 wins $28 + 21 + 24(.024) \approx 49.6$ of its points, each of which is 24% above their 60-40 entitlements. This 3:2 point allocation is also efficient and—what is probably even more important in a bargaining setting dominated by strong personalities—envy-free in an extended sense: Even though company 2 receives slightly less than half of all its points (49.6), it would not envy the two-thirds of company 1's points, which represent $(2/3)(51.4) = 34.4$ of its points, that it is proper to compare its share with (because company 2 is entitled to two-thirds of what company 1 is entitled to).

The indivisibility problem is potentially serious, but it can be successfully dealt with in most merger negotiations in a variety of ways. The second problem is of less moment—the potential for manipulation is very remote and, therefore, unlikely to be a serious obstacle to the implementation of AW. Let's discuss each problem in turn.

INDIVISIBILITY

One way the indivisibility problem can be addressed is already familiar: The parties agree in advance on what it means to receive a given percentage of the equitability-adjustment issue (for example, 60% in a 60-40 split of that issue). But which side receives this larger amount would remain secret.

Thus, if it has been determined that the issue subject to the equitability adjustment is who will be chairman of the surviving company, the parties might agree that receiving 40% on this issue (that is, being the relative loser) means nominating the chairman for the first four years after the merger, whereas receiving 60% (being the relative winner) means nominating the chairman thereafter. This is somewhat similar to divide-and-choose, except that both parties (not just the divider) must agree that the 60-40 split is an equitable one.

As a second approach to dividing an issue, the parties might agree that winning on one or more collateral issues, which are not included in the AW division, may constitute sufficient compensation for letting one of the parties win the entire issue on which the equitability adjustment is to be made. This technique becomes especially appealing if only a small percentage of an issue needs to be transferred from one party to the other.

For example, suppose that the issue subject to the equitability adjustment is once again the chairmanship of the company, but now assume that only 5% of this issue has to be given up by the initial winner. The parties might agree that the initial winner would nominate the chairman in perpetuity and the other party, in return for this concession, would get to select a law firm to serve as an outside general counsel to the merged company (the latter issue, presumably, would be relatively inconsequential and would, therefore, be outside the scope of AW).

Although such negotiations might become more complicated than those in which the equitability-adjustment issue is readily divisible, they would certainly be easier than having no starting point to decide, for example, who is more entitled to get the chairmanship. While the *New York Times* reported that sometimes a chairmanship has been successfully shared between the

CEOs of two merged companies, more often than not "two can be a crowd."

Reaching agreement on an equitability-adjustment issue like the chairmanship may well require that the relative winner compensate, in some form, the relative loser. Without knowing beforehand which party won or lost, each side would not know whether the compensation agreed to would be subtracted from its payoff (if its CEO assumes the chairmanship) or be added to its payoff (if its CEO takes a bow).

As a third approach to dividing an issue, the parties might agree to let a mutually acceptable arbitrator decide what it means to get a specified percentage of the chairmanship or another indivisible issue. Once again, the advantage offered by AW is that only one issue will have to be resolved by the arbitrator.

A fourth approach would be to perform the equitability adjustment on an issue that *is* easily divisible, such as layoffs, even though the ratio of the parties' valuations for that issue is not the smallest. The obvious drawback of doing this is that the resulting allocation would not be efficient; this sacrifice in efficiency, however, would be relatively small if the ratio of valuations is almost the smallest. In that case, the parties might prefer to forego some efficiency gains for the sake of producing an allocation that is both equitable and envy-free.

INSIDE INFORMATION

We saw in Chapter 5 that if one party has precise knowledge of the other party's valuations, AW is manipulable. Short of having this inside information, however, manipulation can fail miserably. While theoretically possible, however, the exploitation of one party by the other is exceedingly unlikely to take place in most merger settings—except, of course, in the extreme case where one company has a spy in the other's camp.

In general, however, it is more realistic to assume that the companies have roughly similar knowledge about each other's valuations. In that case, each company might be tempted to exploit the other, but to do so each would have to predict not only the other company's true valuations but also what valuations the other company might insincerely report in trying to be exploitative itself. The companies' interaction in this scenario would involve a potentially infinite series of guesses and counterguesses about each's best responses and counterresponses.

Worse, manipulative strategies provide no assurance of envyfreeness. It seems likely, therefore, that truthful, or almost truthful, revelation of preferences would be in the companies' interests most of the time, motivating them to be essentially sincere in their point allocations. Thus, unless one company suspects that the other has a spy in its camp (a suspicion that in and of itself should call the feasibility of the deal into question), for all intents and purposes AW can be considered manipulationproof.

In spite of the crucial importance of social issues in mergers, deal makers lack effective tools for their resolution. This problem will not disappear. In April 1998, Wall Street was rocked by news of the $70 billion blockbuster merger between Travelers and Citicorp, which was quickly followed by several other gigantic mergers in the financial-services and other industries, including the $80 billion merger of Exxon and Mobil in November 1998.

These deals highlight the need for effective dispute-resolution techniques in merger negotiations. This is especially true for teasing out agreement on social issues, such as the naming of the new company. In this regard, the *Wall Street Journal* story in May 1998 on the naming of the merged company that combined Daimler-Benz and Chrysler is revealing:

> The matter of the name was "the very last issue" addressed, Mr. Eaton [Robert Eaton, the Chrysler chairman] says. It also was one of the toughest, seeming to focus all the larger doubts and worries inherent in such a giant international transaction. "It was a very emotional issue at the end, emotional on both sides," Mr. Schrempp [Juergen Schrempp, the Daimer-Benz chairman] acknowledges in an interview. "We both felt strongly."
>
> Chrysler executives proposed Chrysler Daimler-Benz. Their German counterparts pushed for Daimler-Benz Chrysler. Both sides had reason to be deeply attached to their names. The German company's two founders were Gottlieb Daimler and

Carl Benz. Walter P. Chrysler, a legendary Detroit automotive pioneer, largely created Chrysler Corp. in 1925 from the wreckage of failed predecessors. The name problem "wasn't a deal breaker," says Mr. Schrempp. "But there was a standoff."

Finally, on Tuesday, they agreed on DaimlerChrysler [without a hyphen to make the merged company sound more like a single entity]. "It looks great and had a lot of class to it," Mr. Eaton says.

Mr. Schrempp says the two companies never considered devising an entirely new name such as Novartis or Diageo. "We are in a business of emotions. Daimler and Chrysler are historical names and mean something" to both customers and employees, he says.

While not providing a panacea to the problem of negotiating over social issues in a merger, AW can help deal makers reach agreement on their fair division. In a setting wherein each negotiator prides himself or herself on the ability to obtain the best possible deal, an allocation that is *not* envy-free, efficient, and equitable would either (1) not be accepted at all or (2) be potentially disruptive of the parties' working relationship in the future. In either case, shareholder value could be obliterated in a standoff between powerful executives used to getting their ways. AW offers a strikingly simple procedure to break this impasse.

THE SPRATLY ISLANDS DISPUTE

Our second case is different, in kind, from the merger case, which concerned determining who would win, perhaps partially, on each of the issues that divided the two sides. The present case harks back to the Camp David case in Chapter 6 and the divorce cases in Chapter 7, because it involves the division of property.

But unlike these settlements, the outcome in the Spratly Islands dispute is not yet known, though the territory that will be allocated or possibly shared is known. In addition, the goals of the parties are not at all transparent. Consequently, it makes sense to postulate a few different scenarios that might be played out.

What is the territory in dispute? It is a group of over 230 small islands and reefs in the South China Sea, which are shown schematically in the map below (ignore for now the lines dividing these islands into different zones).

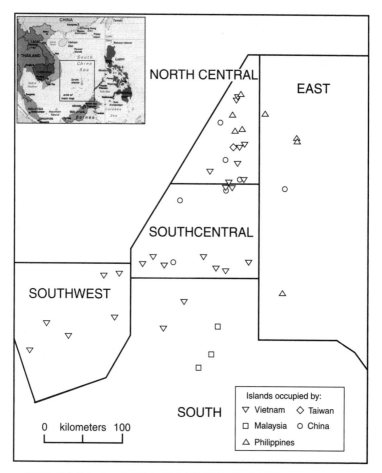

Source: *U.S. Department of State Map # B01010. March 1995.*

The People's Republic of China and the Republic of China—referred to here as China and Taiwan, respectively—and four members of the Association of Southeast Asian Nations

(ASEAN)—Vietnam, the Philippines, Malaysia, and Brunei—have made claims on part or all of the land areas and surrounding waters of the Spratlys. There have been armed clashes in the region over the islands, and the controversy has heated up because of the possibility of major oil and gas deposits in the seabed.

Although the conflicts between the two Koreas and the two Chinas have been more prominent than the conflict over the Spratlys, the latter dispute could, over time, become the most significant international dispute in Asia. The scramble for territory by the various claimants has been fueled by an increasing recognition by the disputants of the economic potential of the Spratlys, including fishing opportunities, which have already precipitated some clashes.

But there is little doubt that the overwhelming economic potential of the Spratlys lies in its hydrocarbons. In July 1995, China's *People's Daily* referred to the South China Sea as "the second Persian Gulf." While this is almost certainly an exaggeration, both exploratory drilling and some oil and gas discoveries indicate that deposits in the Spratlys are likely to be substantial. However, their economic viability is not clear because of the need for building very expensive deep-sea platforms, which could cost as much as $1 billion per site, to extract these resources.

There has been much discussion of the claims of the different disputants as well as the possible role of the International Court of Justice and other agencies in adjudicating these claims. (For example, Indonesia, which has no claims, has convened several working groups to deal with certain technical issues.) While numerous and overlapping claims have been made of the islands, no single country has had continuous possession of any substantial portion of the Spratlys.

It seems unlikely that international legal procedures can quickly resolve the dispute. As one analyst averred,

> The prospect of the law of the sea providing the key to resolution of the [Spratly] dispute is limited, even though each of the protagonists variously refers to the 1982 United Nations Convention of the Law of the Sea to support its claims.

The four major issues that the dispute revolves around are sovereignty, economic development, freedom of passage, and regional security, to which AW, in theory, could be applied to help resolve. However, the key to the settlement of the dispute is sovereignty—who will have control over what islands—and AW would seem to offer a way to facilitate the physical division of the islands among the claimants.

An immediate difficulty in applying AW is that there are more than two parties. This difficulty can be sidestepped for the moment if we regard the conflict as one between China and ASEAN (with ASEAN being considered as a single player, even though two of its members, Singapore and Thailand, are not claimants; also, it is uncertain on what terms Indonesia would be involved).

This view seems realistic as a first step to resolving the overall dispute. China is by far the largest single claimant, against which the ASEAN countries have formed an implicit coalition. (Taiwan's claims overlap China's; how their differences might be resolved in the future will not be considered. While both countries continue to assert that each is the only legitimate China, it is the People's Republic that is the formidable power and, presumably, the "real" player here.)

Although China and ASEAN now control most of the Spratlys, ASEAN political leaders are well aware that China's power and influence are likely to grow over time, so bargaining now (and as an ASEAN group) has advantages. Later we will see how the ASEAN countries might, internally, settle their own competing claims.

Negotiations also seem advantageous for China. True, no Chinese political leader wants to be known as the person who negotiated away "Chinese territory." And if dominance over the South China Sea is an important military objective for China, it would be inadvisable for China to compromise on its claims now. Nonetheless, for China, several factors might tip the balance in favor of attempting to negotiate a settlement soon:

1. China's rapid economic growth will soon necessitate increas-

ing its energy imports, which would be reduced if the hydrocarbons in the Spratlys could be quickly exploited.

2. China's assertiveness in the South China Sea frightens its neighbors and legitimizes the continuing U.S. military role in East Asia, which would likely be diminished without this threat (particularly U.S. naval forces).

3. China's handling of its other border disputes, especially with Vietnam, are rendered more difficult if it takes a rigid stance on the Spratlys.

For the foregoing reasons, it would appear to be in the long-term interest of both China and the ASEAN claimants to try to reach a fair settlement of the Spratlys. A settlement might entail not only partition of the islands but also joint jurisdiction and development of at least some islands, especially those in which both sides have a more-or-less equal interest and where both can benefit from sharing, which AW permits through the equitability adjustment.

Suppose in the subsequent analysis that China and ASEAN are equal claimants, which is a reasonable starting point. However, this supposition could be changed, subject to agreement by the parties, to reflect unequal entitlements, as illustrated in Chapter 5 and in the merger example.

In the Spratly dispute, let's assume that the goods that the two sides must divide are five groups of islands, and adjacent maritime areas, in different parts of the South China Sea: North Central, South Central, East, South, and Southwest (separated by lines in the map on page 134). This division into zones simplifies the allocation problem to one of more manageable proportions than giving each side, say, 1,000 points to distribute over 230 islands and reefs, though it entails some loss due to bundling (more trade-offs are possible with more items).

How China and the ASEAN countries would allocate their points depends upon the goals they seek to maximize. Not having a good fix on exactly what the two sides most desire, let's posit three alternative goals for China, and two for the ASEAN countries, in applying AW.

SCENARIOS FOR CHINA BASED ON GOALS
IT MAY WISH TO MAXIMIZE

1. *Political cooperation.* China seeks to establish its sovereignty in the region but minimize antagonisms with the ASEAN countries. Thus, China gives priority to gaining control of the zones closest to it, North Central and South Central—by placing 40 and 30 points, respectively, on these—and moving less aggressively on the East, South, and Southwest zones by bidding only 10 points each for these.
2. *Military prominence.* China seeks to secure bases in the North Central, South, and Southwest as a means to project its power throughout the entire region. Accordingly, it places 30, 30, and 40 points, respectively, on these three zones but no points on the South Central and East zones.
3. *Economic gain.* China seeks to control the zones with the most promising hydrocarbon deposits (the South and, especially, the Southwest) by placing 30 and 50 points, respectively, on them. It reserves 20 points to try to gain control of the more proximate North Central zone.

SCENARIOS FOR ASEAN BASED ON GOALS
IT MAY WISH TO MAXIMIZE

1. *Political cooperation and economic gain.* ASEAN avoids intruding on the zones closest to China while making strong bids for the South and Southwest, which have the greatest economic potential, by placing 40 points each on these. A modest bid for the East (20 points)—which China was willing to give up on completely in two of its three scenarios—is also a feature of this scenario.
2. *Concentration of control.* ASEAN cedes political control in the North Central and economic control in the Southwest to China. By concentrating its points on the South Central, East, and South—with allocations of 30, 30, and 40 points, respectively—ASEAN tries to force China into noncontiguous zones, thereby impeding China's politico-military hegemony over the entire South China Sea.

These scenarios for China and ASEAN are summarized below:

Region	China			ASEAN	
	1. Political Cooperation	2. Military Prominence	3. Economic Gain	1. Political Cooperation and Economic Gain	2. Concentration of Control
North Central	40	30	20	0	0
South Central	30	0	0	0	30
East	10	0	0	20	30
South	10	30	30	40	40
Southwest	10	40	50	40	0
Total	100	100	100	100	100

Scenarios for China and ASEAN Countries

Pairing off each of China's three scenarios with ASEAN's two scenarios gives six combinations. AW has been applied to each.

Because the two sides have been allowed to allocate 0 points to a region instead of the minimum of 1 point previously assumed, there are some small complications in applying AW. Consider, as an example, the combination of the second goal of China (military prominence) and the first of ASEAN (political cooperation and economic gain). China wins, initially, on North Central (30 to 0); there is a tie on South Central (0 to 0); ASEAN wins on the East (20 to 0) and the South (40 to 30); and there is a tie on the Southwest (40 to 40). Ignoring ties for the moment, China wins on one zone, worth 30 points to it, whereas ASEAN wins on two zones, worth 60 (20 + 40) points to it.

AW awards ties, initially, to the loser, which is China with 30 points. But awarding 40 points on the Southwest to China would give it 70 points, putting it above ASEAN's 60 points. (The other tied zone is the South Central, on which both sides put 0 points, but because of its lack of value to either side, it can be ignored.) Accordingly, there must be an equitability adjustment on the Southwest.

Let x denote the fraction of this zone that ASEAN will receive. Setting ASEAN's points equal to China's yields

$$60 + 40x = 70 - 40x.$$

Solving for x gives

$$80x = 10$$
$$x = \frac{1}{8} = .125.$$

Thus, ASEAN would get 12.5% of the Southwest and China 87.5%.

The reason one generally requires that each side put a minimum of 1 point on each item (zone in this case) is to avoid having to divide by 0 in making comparisons of smallest ratios. Thus, the ratio of points on the tied South Central zone is %, which is undefined; on the East, it is $\frac{20}{0}$%, which is infinite. These zones did not figure in the equitability adjustment, because the first was uncontested and the second would be the last on any smallest-ratio list.

In this example, the minimum-point requirement was ignored to emphasize that each side might be willing to cede control of a zone entirely in order to maximize the number of points it puts on other zones. This requirement, nevertheless, is generally a useful one to stick with because of the calculational problems.

In the first combination shown in the table below (China's goal 1, ASEAN's goal 1), which is given as (C1, A1) in the table, the initial allocation is 70 points to China and 100 points to ASEAN. By giving back the East, which is the smallest-ratio item ($\frac{20}{10} = 2$, compared with $\frac{40}{10} = 4$ each for the South and Southwest), ASEAN decreases its point total from 100 to 80 points, whereas China increases its total from 70 to 80 points. Hence, the giveback of all of the East creates equitability in this case.

The AW allocations for the six combinations are given below:

Region	(C1, A1)	(C1, A2)	(C2, A1)	(C2, A2)	(C3, A1)	(C3, A2)
North Central	C	C	C	C	C	C
South Central	C	$\frac{5}{6}$C, $\frac{1}{6}$A	—	A	—	A
East	C	A	A	A	A	A
South	A	A	A	$\frac{3}{7}$C, $\frac{4}{7}$A	A	$\frac{3}{7}$C, $\frac{4}{7}$A
Southwest	A	C	$\frac{7}{8}$C, $\frac{1}{8}$A	C	$\frac{8}{9}$C, $\frac{1}{9}$A	C
Points (for each party)	80	75	65	82.9	64.4	82.9

Winners and Partial Winners for Six China-ASEAN Combinations

Note: C=China; A=ASEAN. The number following each letter indicates the one (of three) possible goals of China and the one (of two) possible goals of ASEAN, as described in text.

Notice in the (C1, A1) case that how much the initial winner, ASEAN, loses (20 points) is not how much the initial loser, China, gains (10 points) in the giveback. There will be equality in the giveback to the two parties only if there is a tie in the points that the two sides allocate to the zones, as was true in our earlier (C2, A1) example.

In all except the case of (C1, A1), there is an equitability adjustment involving a split; because this adjustment occurs on the one zone that the two sides value most equally (in ratio terms), it has the strongest claim for being the zone over which the two sides *should* share control.

Practically speaking, what might such sharing mean? As an example, take the case of (C2, A1) discussed earlier, in which the Southwest is divided in the ratio 7:1. Which side is entitled to what islands? This question would be especially difficult to answer if there were hydrocarbon deposits near some islands but not others.

Alternatively, the two sides might agree on joint control of the islands and then negotiate a production and revenue-sharing agreement, based on the 7:1 ratio. Whether the two sides physically divide the islands or the revenues in this ratio, the approach discussed in earlier cases could be used.

To wit, a referee or mediator administering AW would tell the two sides that there would be a relative winner, getting seven-eighths, and a relative loser, getting one-eighth—but not which side is the winner. Here the disputants would be asked to formulate one agreement, specifying what the seven-eighths winner and the one-eighth loser would receive. Only after there was agreement would the parties be told which side was the winner and which side the loser, and therefore which would get the lion's share.

Except for the zone on which there is an equitability adjustment, let's assume that each side gains complete sovereignty over all islands in the zone it wins. This is not to say, however, that joint development agreements would be ruled out. Indeed, they might prove extremely attractive if a promising field overlapped two zones.

The winners and partial winners for the six combinations show that each side benefits substantially under AW. Depending upon the combination of bids, both China and ASEAN realize between 64% and 83% of their objectives. Even in the worst case of (C3, A1), each side gets almost two-thirds of all the zones as it values them.

It should be noted that certain situational factors, like geographic proximity, may help the ASEAN claimants reach a settlement. For example, there are clear natural divisions, based on proximity, within ASEAN, suggesting, on first cut, the East for the Philippines, the South for Malaysia and Brunei, and the Southwest for Vietnam. To be sure, these allocations will depend upon the outcome of the China-ASEAN division, on which each of the ASEAN claimants would presumably have some say.

Of course, our AW scenarios for China and ASEAN are meant to be illustrative—even Asian specialists do not know exactly what priority each side would attach to the different goals postulated (and perhaps other goals not postulated). While the postulated goals for the Spratly parties are defensible, it is likely, especially for ASEAN, that its actual bidding strategies might reflect a blend of goals, including some we have not identified.

This blending, of course, would produce different allocations. However, our main purpose is not to say what the "true" valuations of China and ASEAN—or any of the parties in the other cases—are but, rather, to recommend a *methodology* for reaching a fair settlement, as was our goal in the merger and earlier cases. Consequently, our analysis does not stand or fall on substantive disagreements about either the point allocations or the goals that underlie them.

A final question remains: How should one deal with the three other major issues involved in the Spratly Islands dispute—freedom of passage, economic development, and regional security? As with the sovereignty issue, AW could be used to determine who wins, relatively speaking, on different components of each issue. But these other issues are probably not so amenable to AW until questions of sovereignty are resolved.

Chapter 9
WHICH PROCEDURE IS BEST?

Each of the procedures we've examined in this book seems well suited for different situations. Let's see which ones are most appropriate in what circumstances.

NON-ADJUSTED WINNER PROCEDURES

- *Balanced alternation is simple to use.* Strict alternation is probably the most commonly applied procedure in divorce and estate division, but it introduces a first-chooser bias that can lead to envy unless all items are valued about the same. Balanced alternation, on the other hand, enables the parties to surmount the first-chooser bias in many cases. If there are a large number of relatively small items, or if the parties are unable or unwilling to compare collections (as required by divide-and-choose) or to quantify preferences by assigning points (as required by AW), then balanced alternation is not only simple to use but also difficult to manipulate. On the other hand, if issues—particularly if they are intangible—are being negotiated rather than goods, alternating procedures make little sense. Taking turns on who prevails, issue by issue, is too crude a device to produce a refined and subtle balancing of interests.
- *Divide-and-choose is seldom the best choice, but it has merit in certain situations.* Divide-and-choose has an ancient pedigree, and there are situations—like physically dividing a cake, or land tracts for undersea mining—to which it is applicable and for which neither balanced alternation nor AW can be used. Divide-and-choose may also be sensible in the equitability-adjustment phase of AW. If a relative loser's proportion of an item can be approximated by fractions such as one-half, one-fourth, one-eighth, and so on, these portions can be obtained by repeated application of divide-and-choose. Generally

speaking, however, it is not easy for a divider to construct two equal piles; this effort would be better spent on AW, which also requires quantification but leads to an envy-free, efficient, and equitable allocation.

- *Balanced alternation and divide-and-choose both have useful extensions to three or more parties.* Little is lost in going from two to three or more parties with balanced alternation. It is still simple to use and fair in most situations. Divide-and-choose, by comparison, can become quite complicated if there are three parties, although its extension (the trimming procedure) is based on the same simple idea that underlies divide-and-choose: One person creates several equal packages (in terms of his or her valuations), and other people create equality by trimming. Like divide-and-choose, the trimming procedure leads to an envy-free allocation. Envy-freeness is particularly important in emotionally charged situations, such as those one finds in families in which an estate is being divided up among several family members and feelings of envy can be explosive. To use the trimming procedure effectively, however, it is helpful to have a number of small items that can be shifted around between packages, or pared off from them, to create equality.

ADJUSTED WINNER

- *AW is easily applied to goods but less easily to issues, in which much negotiation must precede its use.* In applying AW to goods in, say, a divorce or estate division, the only real difficulty is in each person's assigning points to the goods. If the items are not physical goods but issues that must be resolved, then the parties need to reach agreement—before the application of AW can even begin—on what the issues are and what winning and losing on each issue means. Because there is no mechanical procedure that can resolve differences at this level, this is the area in which a good deal of hard bargaining is to be expected.
- *The packaging of issues is crucial in applying AW, particularly in breaking up a single large issue into different parts that*

are as separable as possible. Thus, if salary is the overriding concern in a labor-management dispute, then there is nothing to trade off against losing on this issue. But often an issue like this can be broken down into components, such as basic hourly or piecework rate, overtime wages, pensions, medical benefits, and the like that the employer and the employee value differently. Hence, "salary" is turned into a compensation package, and its components can be treated as separate issues. Care must be taken in packaging items, however, so as to make them relatively independent of each other. This is to ensure that winning on one does not affect how much one values another, thereby making the summation of points across all items meaningful.

- *Manipulation is sufficiently difficult under AW so as not to be a practical problem.* One catch in using AW is that, theoretically, one side can do even better, at the expense of the other side, by capitalizing on its advance knowledge of the other side's allocations. This is not a serious practical problem, however, because it is highly unlikely that one side would have the precise information it needs about the other side's allocations to exploit AW in this manner. In fact, although being off by only one point can lead to a relatively poor outcome for both parties, the honest party's sincerity guarantees that it will not envy the disingenuous party. Thus, the incentives to exploit AW will be minimal, with honesty guaranteeing a party at least half the total value of all items.

WHICH ONE TO PICK

- *AW is a better procedure than divide-and-choose in most situations.* This will be especially true in situations in which there are multiple goods or issues, and the parties value them differently from one another. Then AW will produce not only a division that is envy-free and efficient but also one that is equitable in the sense of equalizing the surpluses over 50% that each party receives. This result obviates the kind of second-order envy expressed when a husband complains, "While I got

51 percent of what I wanted, my wife walked away with 90 percent of what she wanted." Inequitability can embitter a person—for example, the husband in a divorce—even though he gets more than one-half of the total in his view (51% in the above example). While devoid of envy, he may be furious that his wife is far happier with her share than he is with his. In our earlier examples, by comparison, both sides often ended up with about two-thirds to three-quarters of the total, in their own views. Moreover, because AW is efficient, this was the best that the two sides could possibly do.

- *Balanced alternation is a more practicable procedure than AW in two-person disputes that involve many relatively small items.* This proposition might apply to a young urban professional couple without children that has no shared possessions of great value. Thus, for example, many such couples who rent apartments in New York City do not own a car or even a washing machine and a dryer. But when they get divorced, they still must decide who will get the exercise machine, television, CD player, bed, bookcases, computer equipment, and many other things. The query step will separate the items that are contested from those that are not, expediting a settlement. Allocating points under AW may simply not be worth the bother, especially because balanced alternation makes up for the fact that one player gets first choice. Unless our couple is devious or spiteful, each person will simply choose the best one or two items available when his or her turn comes up.

- *All the procedures are applicable when entitlements are unequal, and if the division is of losses (bads) as well as gains (goods).* Entitlements can be incorporated into AW by altering its basic calculation so as to enable one party to receive, for example, twice as many points as the other. In the case of the alternating or trimming procedures, single parties can be replaced by clones that reflect the different proportions to which each party is entitled. For example, two clones could replace a single party that is entitled to twice as much as another party. In dividing up bad things like chores, the interpretation of winning under AW can simply be reversed, whereby it means one does not have to accept the chore one "wins"—the other party gets it. Under strict or balanced alternation, chore division is likewise straightforward: One would choose the least-bad item first. In disputes, it seems fair to say, the division of bads may be as important as the division of goods. Besides household chores (who does the dishes or who mows the lawn), bads may range from business tasks (who assumes what extra work when there is downsizing) to international burdens (who defends what vulnerable positions in a military alliance).

Bads aside, the good news is this:

- Balanced alternation enables the disputants to go beyond the favoritism of strict alternation, in which the first chooser starts with a lead that he or she never has to give up;
- AW enables the disputants to go beyond divide-and-choose, which guarantees envy-freeness but neither efficiency nor equitability.

Not only do these two new procedures apply to many fair-division disputes, but they also are not difficult to understand or to use.

There are few guarantees in life. Fairness should be one of them. Don't settle for less.

GLOSSARY

Adjusted winner (AW). Adjusted winner is a two-person point-allocation procedure that is envy-free, efficient, and equitable if the parties are truthful in their point allocations.

Arbitration. Arbitration of a dispute involves its resolution by an outside party (arbitrator), who makes a decision about the terms of a settlement that is binding on the disputants.

Alternation procedure. An alternating procedure is one in which the parties take turns choosing items, though not necessarily by choosing one item at a time.

Balanced alternation. Balanced alternation is a modification of strict alternation, in which the parties take turns taking turns taking turns. . . .

BATNA. BATNA is the abbreviation for *B*est *A*lternative *T*o a *N*egotiated *A*greement, or a party's fallback position. While meaningful in disputes in which a party can afford to walk away from the bargaining table, it is not meaningful in other disputes, such as divorce, labor-management, and international conflicts, in which the disputants have little recourse but to try to reach a fair settlement.

Bottom-up strategy. A bottom-up strategy is a strategy under an alternating procedure in which sophisticated choices are determined by working backward.

Chores problem. The chores problem is the opposite of dividing up goods. The objective is to give parties as few chores (or bads) as possible so that the resulting allocation satisfies certain properties of fairness.

Contested pile. Items that are contested as a result of the query step are put into the contested pile; these items will be ranked by the parties from best to worst in exactly the same way.

Divide-and-choose. Divide-and-choose is a two-person procedure, applicable to one or more goods, in which one party (the divider) divides the good (or goods) into two pieces, and the other party (the chooser) selects one of the pieces. The procedure is envy-free but not efficient, assuming that the divider has no information about the chooser's preferences and makes the division 50-50 in his or her estimation.

Divisible good. A good is divisible if it can be divided into parts without destroying the value of its parts to the parties.

Efficiency. An allocation is efficient if there is no other allocation that is better for some party without being worse for some other party.

Entitlement. The entitlement of a party specifies the minimum proportion of an item or items that it should receive under a fair-division procedure.

Envy-freeness. An allocation is envy-free if each party thinks it receives a portion that is at least as valuable as the portion received by every other party.

Equitability. An allocation is equitable if each party believes it received the same fractional part of the total value.

Equitability adjustment. Under adjusted winner, the equitability adjustment equalizes the point totals of the two disputants, starting with the smallest-ratio item.

Fairness. A procedure is fair to the degree that it satisfies certain properties—in particular, envy-freeness, efficiency, and equitability—enabling each party to achieve a certain level of satisfaction regardless of what the other parties do.

Guarantee strategy. A guarantee strategy is a strategy that a party can choose such that no matter what strategies the other parties choose, this party can guarantee that its portion satisfies certain properties (for example, envy-freeness).

Heterogeneous good. A heterogeneous good is a good that is not the same throughout; hence, different parties may value portions of it differently.

Homogeneous good. A homogeneous good is the same throughout, so all parties value portions of it the same.

Impartial procedure. An impartial procedure is one that does not favor a particular party.

Indivisible good. An indivisible good is one that cannot be divided without destroying its value.

Item. An item is either a good or an issue, and it may be divisible or indivisible.

Item-by-item comparison. Item-by-item comparison is used to compare collections of items with respect to envy-freeness, efficiency, and equitability by comparing each item in one collection with each item in another collection.

Manipulability. A procedure is manipulable to the degree that parties can, by knowing the preferences of other parties, exploit that knowledge to obtain a larger portion of a collection than they can obtain by not having this knowledge.

Mediation. Mediation of a dispute involves an outside party (mediator), who helps the disputants clarify their objectives, better communicate with each other, reduce tensions, and so on in order to facilitate the settlement of a dispute.

Moving-finger procedure. The moving-finger procedure is a symmetricized version of divide-and-choose, involving a finger moving down a list of items that, after transfers and trades, leads to a division of the items that both parties view as approximately 50-50.

Point-allocation procedure. A point-allocation procedure is a procedure under which parties can allocate a fixed number of points (for example, 100) to different items that reflects, if they are truthful, the relative importance they attach to receiving them.

Proportionality. An allocation is proportional if every one of n parties thinks it received a portion that is worth at least $1/n$ of the total value.

Query step. In strict or balanced alternation, a query step involves asking the parties what item they would next choose.

Referee. A referee is a person who ensures that the rules of a procedure are followed.

Rules. Rules describe the legal choices that parties can make under a procedure, which can be enforced by a referee who does not know their preferences.

Separability. Goods or issues are separable if the values that parties attach to them are independent of the parties' possessing other goods or winning on other issues.

Sincere strategy. A sincere strategy is a course of action that is based solely on a party's truthful preferences.

Smallest-ratio item. Under adjusted winner, the smallest-ratio item is the item that is first given in whole or part to the initial loser to achieve equitability.

Social issues. Social issues in mergers concern matters of status, role, and prestige in the merged company.

Sophisticated strategy. A sophisticated strategy is one that takes account of how other parties will act, based on their preferences, in deciding upon one's own optimal choice.

Strategy. A strategy is a course of action a party chooses that is consistent with a procedure's rules.

Strict alternation. Strict alternation is a procedure in which first one party chooses an item, then another party does, and so on, until all the items are exhausted.

Taking turns taking turns taking turns . . . Parties take turns going first in a sequence of steps. For example, the sequence Ann-Ben is "taking turns," or *one turn*, with Ann going first; Ann-Ben-Ben-Ann is "taking turns taking turns," or *two turns*, with Ann going first in the first sequence (Ann-Ben) and Ben going first in the second sequence (Ben-Ann). This process can be extended to three turns, four turns, and so on with two or more people.

Trimming procedure. The trimming procedure is a procedure whereby parties trim larger piles of items, in terms of value, down to smaller piles, enabling the parties to create piles of equal value, which can ensure envy-freeness but cannot ensure efficiency.

Valuation. A party's valuation is the fraction of the total value that it attaches to obtaining each good or winning on each issue.

SOURCES

CHAPTER 1

FAIR-DIVISION STORIES

For information on the Wendt divorce case, see Bumiller (1997); Dobrzynski (1997*a*, 1997*b*); Morrow (1997); "Move to Reopen Executive Divorce Case" (1997); Herring (1998); and Morris (1998).

The dispute over Yves Montand's estate is described in Whitney (1998) and "Yves Montand DNA Says No Paternity" (1998). Montand's body was exhumed in March 1998 when his alleged daughter, Aurore, was 22. In a poll conducted by the French Institute of Public Opinion after the Appeals Court ordered Montand's tomb to be opened for a DNA test, 75% of the French public indicated that Montand should not have been made to do something after his death that he would not have done while he was alive. As one French newspaper put it, he was ordered, in effect, to speak from the grave. Aurore said at the time: "I have always been persuaded that my mother has never been lying to me, and deep inside I am sure I am his [Montand's] daughter."

The quotations from *The Harmless People* can be found in Thomas (1959, pp. 49–50).

Gardner (1993, pp. 198, 202) provides the two accounts of discussions between Churchill and Stalin, and Eden and Molotov.

Cordingly (1995, p. 97) discusses the division of loot among pirates.

Pocock (1977, 1992) reprints and discusses James Harrington's writings, including *The Commonwealth of Oceana*; other exegeses of Harrington's work are cited in Brams and Taylor (1996, ch. 1), in which a variation of divide-and-choose, called "filter-and-choose," is analyzed. Harrington's proposal that one party have the ability to veto the choice of another was anticipated in the constitution of Sparta, attributed to Lycurgus (Plutarch's *Lycurgus*, 6.3). While the assembly of Sparta could not make motions, it could accept or reject motions presented to it by the kings and senate. Likewise in Carthage, kings and elders decided what is taken to the people, who then were able to decide what to do (Aristotle's *Politics*, 1237A5f). Plass (1997) called our attention to the precedents of Sparta and Carthage's use of the idea behind Harrington's proposed constitutional reform in seventeenth-century England; see also Plass (1995). In Young (1994, ch. 4), classic fair-division solutions proposed by Aristotle, the Talmud, and the Jewish philosopher, Maimonides, among others, are compared; see Aumann and Maschler (1985) for an enlightening game-theoretic interpretation of a Talmudic rule for apportioning the debt in a bankruptcy.

Lowry (1987, p. 130) is the source of the first Aesop fable (the second was referred to us without attribution).

Brams (1980, ch. 6; 1990, ch. 1) analyzed the "game" played between the two mothers in response to King Solomon's edict, and assumed that

- The mother's top priority would be saving her baby, even at the cost of losing him (it was a boy) to the impostor;
- The impostor would disdain saving the baby and instead seek to curry Solomon's favor by not protesting his solution.

Solomon's setup, as described in the text, "worked"—the mother protested and the impostor did not—but only because the women did not discern Solomon's underlying purpose. If the impostor, in particular, had been more perspicacious, then she, like the mother, would have protested, leaving Solomon in a quandary about who the true mother was. Then his solution would have appeared less dazzling, and Solomon less brilliant. While Solomon is revered for his exemplary judgment, there is no question that his setup involved deception. He should perhaps be extolled as much for his cunning in deceiving the impostor as for his probity in finding a just solution. Presumably, one would not applaud this kind of cunning were it used by unscrupulous people, without the judicious temperament of Solomon, to extract information for untoward purposes.

CRITERIA OF SATISFACTION

Proportionality is a key concept in apportioning seats to states in a legislature (Balinski and Young, 1982) and in apportioning weighted votes to different-sized jurisdictions in a council (Felsenthal and Machover, 1998).

RULES AND STRATEGIES

Brams and Kilgour (1998) provide a model of fallback bargaining based on BATNAs, which might include continuing impasse. The quotation from *Models of My Life* is from Simon (1991, pp. 365–366).

CHAPTER 2

THE BOTTOM-UP STRATEGY

Kohler and Chandrasekaran (1971) prove that the bottom-up strategy (not their terminology) yields optimal strategic choices for two parties.

ASSESSMENT

Brams and Straffin (1979) prove that sophisticated choices for two parties, and sincere choices for any number of parties, are efficient.

EXTENSIONS TO THREE OR MORE PARTIES

Brams and Straffin (1979) analyze in detail the three-person Prisoners' Dilemma example used in the text and discuss the paradox of player selection, the paradox of team selection, and the nonuniqueness of the sophisticated outcome. For background and further information on the original two-person Prisoners' Dilemma, as well as the theoretical and empirical research it has inspired, see Dixit and Nalebuff (1991), Poundstone (1992), and Taylor (1995).

CHAPTER 3

TAKING TURNS TAKING TURNS TAKING TURNS . . .

Taylor (1998) provides an axiomatic treatment of taking turns and identifies difficulties that can arise in defining fair sequences. Dawson (1997, p. 82) distinguishes between the regular draft and the modified draft.

CHAPTER 4

HISTORY

Lowry (1987, pp. 126–131) discusses at length the problems that plagued the Prometheus-Zeus division of the meat. The quotation from *Memoirs of Reprieve* is from Levi (1979, p. 45). Young (1995, p. 912) recounts how Egypt and the British Museum divided up the archeological finds, crediting economist Thomas C. Schelling as the source.

STRATEGY

The division of the Maine estate is discussed in a somewhat different way by Brams and Taylor (1996, pp. 10–12, 16–18). The commentary on choosing pizza slices as a child is from Alba (1994).

SYMMETRICIZING DIVIDE-AND-CHOOSE

For details on the symmetricizing approach, including the use of "moving knives" to create ties, see Brams and Taylor (1996) and Robertson and Webb (1998); the idea behind it is from Austin (1982). By symmetricizing divide-and-choose through randomized and alternating choices, Dawson (1997) develops a procedure for making sports draft choices more equitable.

EXTENSIONS TO THREE OR MORE PARTIES

Brams and Taylor (1996) present theoretical results that underlie these extensions and also provide an example of estate division among four heirs (pp. 143–147). Smith (1963, pp. 16–17, 28–29) and Sharp (1975) give details of the division of Germany and Berlin into four zones after World War II; the quotation on the Americans and British being at loggerheads is from Eisenberg (1996, pp. 57–58).

RECOMMENDATIONS

Young (1994) discusses and gives example of sharing and rotation as alternatives to the division of items. The quotation from *To Sail Beyond the Sunset* is from Heinlein (1987, p. 248).

CHAPTER 5

IDEA OF ADJUSTED WINNER

Leng and Epstein (1985) and Salter (1986) include details on their point-allocation schemes for arms reductions. The quotation on the issue of being truthful is from Young (1994, p. 130). Brams and Taylor (1996, p. 70, ftn. 8) provide a different example illustrating the application of AW to a case in which two parties have unequal entitlements.

ASSESSMENT

The works of Ralph Keeney and Howard Raiffa, alluded to in the discussion of efficiency, are Keeney and Raiffa (1991) and Raiffa (1985, 1993); more technical treatments can be found in Moulin (1995) and Raiffa (1996). Raith (1998a, 1998b) and Raith and Welzel

(1998) show how AW and modifications of it can be used to implement and support different solutions in cooperative game theory; they also discuss AW's relationship to earlier fair-division schemes.

STRATEGY

Another point-allocation procedure analyzed by Brams and Taylor (1996, chs. 4–5) is "proportional allocation" (PA), which is less vulnerable to misrepresentation than AW. However, it has two strikes against it, the first being that it is not efficient—both parties can, in general, benefit from using AW over PA (Ann and Ben would be reduced from 75 points to 62.5 points under PA in the Matisse-Picasso example). Also, it requires splitting every item according to the proportion of points that each party puts on it and, hence, is not as practicable as AW, which requires splitting only the one item on which there is an equitability adjustment.

EXTENSIONS TO THREE OR MORE PARTIES

The quotation of Harold Nicolson is from Nicolson (1992, p. 83). Extensions of AW to three or more parties are given in Reijnierse and Potters (1998) and Willson (1998).

CHAPTER 6

Negotiation analysis is a term used to describe applications of decision theory and game theory—like that in this chapter—to the study of bargaining and negotiation; it can be found in the titles of works by Young (1991), Sebenius (1992), and Raiffa (1996). Game theory also underlies Brandenburger and Nalebuff's (1996) treatment of "co-opetition," a term they use to indicate how a successful business both cooperates to create a bigger pie and competes to get a bigger share of it. It is worth pointing out that under AW, two parties can do better *without* the pie's expanding if they are truthful—that is, engage in a kind of "honest" competition, eschewing guile in making their point allocations.

The Camp David application is based on Brams and Togman (1996/1998); a related application is provided by Massoud (1998). Other applications of negotiation analysis to international disputes are given by Raiffa (1982), Sebenius (1984), and Brams (1990). Raiffa (1982, ch. 12) is, in fact, the source of point allocations that Brams and Taylor (1996, ch. 5) use in their application of AW to the Panama Canal treaty dispute of the late 1970s.

ISSUES AT CAMP DAVID

The main sources used on Camp David in this section and later in the chapter are Brzezinski (1983), Dayan (1981), Kacowicz (1994), Quandt (1986), Stein (1993), and Telhami (1990). The sources of the quotations are as follows: Carter (1982, p. 294) on the Sadat letter to Carter; Brzezinski (1983, p. 263) on the Begin statement to the American negotiating team; Stein (1993, p. 81) on the primacy that Sadat gave to Israeli withdrawal from the Sinai; Kacowicz (1994, p. 135) on the symbolic value of Sinai to Egypt; Quandt (1986, p. 66) on Begin's inflexibility in relinquishing Judea and Samaria; Carter (1982, p. 345) on Sadat's not signing an agreement; Quandt (1986, p. 161) on Carter's Aswân statement; Dayan (1981, p. 177) on the need to rewrite the Bible; Dayan (1981, p. 49) on the Egyptian representative's statement on Jerusalem; and Kacowicz (1994, p. 139) on Egypt's acknowledgment of Israel's right to the West Bank and Gaza. Brams and Taylor (1996, ch. 5) describe the application of AW to the Panama Canal treaty negotiations, based on data given by Raiffa (1982, ch. 12). Brams (1990, ch. 2) uses game-theoretic bargaining models, based on honesty-inducing "bonus" and "penalty" procedures, to identify the incentives of the adversaries to reach agreement at Camp David; these models are rigorously developed in Brams and Kilgour (1996). Other examples of rational-choice models to interpret history as "analytic narratives" are given in Bates *et al.* (1998).

PRACTICAL CONSIDERATIONS

Raiffa (1982, part III) discusses ways of expressing intensities of preference and making trade-offs; see also Raiffa (1996). Saaty and Vargas (1991) and Saaty (1995) describe and illustrate analytic hierarchy processing. The quotation of Henry Kissinger on the best timing for a settlement comes from the *New York Times*, October 12, 1974; Jimmy Carter's comments appear in Carter (1994, p. 390).

FAIRNESS OF THE CAMP DAVID AGREEMENT

The quotation of Fahmy on Camp David is from Fahmy (1983, p. 292). Quandt's view that Israel did better at Camp David is given in Quandt (1986, p. 255). On the manipulability of procedures generally, see Riker (1986, 1996), Brams (1990), and Brams and Kilgour (1996).

CHAPTER 7

DIVORCE

The Trump divorce case is based on Duran (1995), which was summarized in COMAP (1997). On Marla's separation from Donald, see Weber (1997); the quotation of Donald on this separation is from Singer (1997, p. 58). The quotations of Donald about loving Ivana, and of Ivana about wanting a fair share, are from Mitchell (1990); the quotation of Ivana about being madly in love with Donald is from Gross (1990). The analysts quoted on the problems of using informal processes in divorce are Erlanger, Chambliss, and Melli (1987, p. 583). The example of the father's wanting to keep secret the fact that he put fewer points on a child than did the mother is based on a divorce case analyzed, using AW, by Brams and Taylor (1996, ch. 5). On AW's use in family conflicts generally, see Lavery (1996).

PRESIDENTIAL DEBATES

The presidential-debates case is based on Sims (1996). All the quotations, with one exception, come from Lewis (1996*a*, 1996*b*, 1996*c*); the exception is the quotation about Bob Dole's not being able to afford elimination of the debates, which is given in Black (1996). Lax (1999) proposes that a variant of AW be used in decisions about future presidential debates and illustrates this variant's application in the 1996 case.

CHAPTER 8

For details on the major-league baseball strike and its settlement, see Jennings (1997). Langreth and Lipin (1998) is the source of the quotation about the aborted merger of Glaxo Wellcome and SmithKline Beecham.

MERGERS

The merger example is based on Brams and Kulikov (1998). The Michael Carr quotation is from Lipin (1997); the Robert Kindler quotation is from Lipin (1996). The figure of about $1 trillion in deals in the first half of 1998, as well as an average of 29 deals a day, is also given in Holson (1998). The Mercer Management Consulting study is cited in Ashkens, De Monaco, and Francis (1998). The *New York Times* article on "two can be a crowd" is Bryant (1998). The *Wall Street Journal* article on defections caused by the merger of Swiss

Bank Corporation and Union Bank of Switzerland is Rhoads *et al.* (1998); that on the naming of DaimlerChrysler is Ingrassia and Mitchener (1998); the case is further explored in Ryback (1998).

THE SPRATLY ISLANDS DISPUTE

The Spratly Islands case is based on Denoon and Brams (1997, 1998). The quotation on the Law of the Sea's providing the key to the resolution of the dispute is given in Cordner (1994, p. 61).

REFERENCES

Alba, William (1994). Private communication to Steven J. Brams (December 15).

Ashkens, Ronald N., Lawrence J. De Monaco, and Suzanne C. Francis (1998). "Making the Deal Work: How GE Capital Integrates Acquisitions." *Harvard Business Review* 76, no. 1 (January–February): 165–170.

Aumann, Robert J., and Michael Maschler (1985). "Game Theoretic Analysis of a Bankruptcy Problem in the Talmud." *Journal of Economic Theory* 36, no. 2 (August): 195–213.

Austin, A. K. (1982). "Sharing a Cake." *Mathematical Gazette* 66, no. 437 (October): 212–215.

Balinski, Michel L., and H. Peyton Young (1982). *Fair Representation: Meeting the Ideal of One Man, One Vote.* New Haven, CT: Yale University Press.

Bates, Robert H., *et al.* (1998). *Analytic Narratives.* Princeton, NJ: Princeton University Press.

Black, Gordon S. (1996). "Clinton Should Stand Up for Perot." *New York Times*, September 25, p. A21.

Brams, Steven J. (1980). *Biblical Games: A Strategic Analysis of Stories in the Old Testament.* Cambridge, MA: MIT Press.

Brams, Steven J. (1990). *Negotiation Games: Applying Game Theory to Bargaining and Arbitration.* New York: Routledge.

Brams, Steven J., and D. Marc Kilgour (1996). "Bargaining Procedures That Induce Honesty." *Group Decision and Negotiation* 5: 239–262.

Brams, Steven J., and D. Marc Kilgour (1998). "Fallback Bargaining." Preprint, Department of Politics, New York University.

Brams, Steven J., and Maxim S. Kulikov (1998). "Resolving Social Issues in a Merger: A Fair-Division Approach." Preprint, Department of Politics, New York University.

Brams, Steven J., and Philip D. Straffin, Jr. (1979). "Prisoners' Dilemma and Professional Sports Drafts." *American Mathematical Monthly* 86, no. 2 (February): 80–88.

Brams, Steven J., and Alan D. Taylor (1996). *Fair Division: From*

Cake-Cutting to Dispute Resolution. Cambridge, UK: Cambridge University Press.

Brams, Steven J., and Jeffrey M. Togman (1996/1998). "Camp David: Was the Agreement Fair?" *Conflict Management and Peace Science* 13, no. 3 (1996): 99–112; revised and expanded version in Frank P. Harvey and Ben D. Mor (eds.), *New Directions in the Study of Conflict, Crisis, and War.* London: Macmillan, 1998, pp. 306–323.

Brandenburger, Adam M., and Barry J. Nalebuff (1996). *Co-opetition.* New York: Doubleday.

Bryant, Adam (1998). "Co-Chief Executives: Can Two Be a Crowd?" *New York Times*, August 1, p. BU4.

Brzezinski, Zbigniew (1983). *Power and Principle: Memoirs of the National Security Adviser, 1977–1981.* New York: Farrar Straus Giroux.

Bumiller, Elisabeth (1997). "One Word from a Corporate Ex-Wife: Half." *New York Times*, January 6, p. B2.

Carter, Jimmy (1982). *Keeping Faith: Memoirs of a President.* New York: Bantam.

Carter, Jimmy (1994). "The Power of Moral Suasion in International Mediation." In Deborah M. Kolb *et al.* (eds.), *When Talk Works: Profiles of Mediators.* San Francisco: Jossey-Bass, pp. 375–391.

COMAP (1997). *For All Practical Purposes: Introduction to Contemporary Mathematics*, 4th ed. New York: W. H. Freeman.

Cordingly, David (1995). *Under the Black Flag: The Romance and the Reality of Life Among the Pirates.* New York: Random House.

Cordner, L. (1994). "The Spratlys Dispute and the Law of the Sea." *Ocean Development and International Law* 25: 61.

Dawson, Bryan (1997). "A Better Draft: Fair Division of the Talent Pool." *College Mathematics Journal* 28, no. 2 (March): 82–88.

Dayan, Moshe (1981). *Breakthrough: A Personal Account of the Egypt-Israel Peace Negotiations.* New York: Alfred A. Knopf.

Denoon, David B. H., and Steven J. Brams (1997). "Fair Division: A New Approach to the Spratly Islands Controversy." *International Negotiation* 2, no. 2 (December): 303–329.

Denoon, David, and Stephen J. Brams (1998). "Fair Division: A New Approach to Dispute Resolution." In Gerald Blake *et al.* (eds.), *Boundaries and Energy: Problems and Prospects.* London: Kluwer Law International, pp. 509–519.

Dixit, Avinash, and Barry Nalebuff (1991). *Thinking Strategically: The Competitive Edge in Business, Politics, and Everyday Life.* New York: W. W. Norton.

Dobrzynski, Judith H. (1997a). "Was It His Career, or Theirs? A Corporate Wife Holds Out for a 50-50 Split of Assets." *New York Times*, January 24, p. D16.

Dobrzynski, Judith H. (1997b). "Judge Splits on Issues and Money in G.E. Executive's Divorce Case." *New York Times*, December 4, pp. D1, D8.

Duran, Catherine (1995). "Trump v. Trump: A Fair Division Analysis." Unpublished term paper written for Steven J. Brams, New York University.

Eisenberg, Carolyn Woods (1996). *Drawing the Line: The American Decision to Divide Germany, 1944–1949.* Cambridge, UK: Cambridge University Press.

Erlanger, Howard S., Elizabeth Chambliss, and Marygold S. Melli (1987). "Participation and Flexibility in Informal Processes: Cautions from the Divorce Context." *Law and Society Review* 21, no. 4: 583–604.

Fahmy, Ismail (1983). *Negotiating for Peace in the Middle East.* Baltimore, MD: Johns Hopkins University Press.

Felsenthal, Dan S., and Moshé Machover (1998). *The Measurement of Voting Power.* Cheltenham, UK: Edward Elgar.

Fisher, Roger, and William Ury (1981). *Getting to Yes: Negotiating Agreement Without Giving In.* Boston: Houghton Mifflin (2d ed., Penguin, 1991).

Gardner, Lloyd C. (1993). *Spheres of Influence: The Great Powers Partition Europe, from Munich to Yalta.* Chicago: Ivan R. Dee.

Gross, Michael (1990). "Ivana's New Life." *New York* 23, no. 4 (October 15): 40.

Heinlein, Robert A. (1987). *To Sail Beyond the Sunset: The Life and Loves of Maureen Johnson (Being the Memoirs of a Somewhat Irregular Lady).* New York: Berkley.

Herring, Hubert B. (1998). "What's a Corporate Wife Worth in Court? Go Figure." *New York Times*, January 25, p. WK7.

Holson, Laura M. (1998). "The Incredible Shrinking Banker." *New York Times*, August 2, pp. BU2, BU9.

The Honeymooners (1955). "One Big Happy Family" (aired on CBS on April 9). A Jackie Gleason, Inc., Production.

Ingrassia, Lawrence, and Brandon Mitchener (1998). "I Was Thinking That, Too, Said Mr. Eaton—And the Talks Were On." *Wall Street Journal*, May 8, pp. A1, A10.

Jennings, Kenneth M. (1997). *Swings and Misses: Moribund Labor Relations in Professional Baseball.* Westport, CT: Praeger.

Kacowicz, Arie Marcelo (1994). *Peaceful Territorial Change.* Columbia, SC: University of South Carolina Press.

Keeney, Ralph L., and Howard Raiffa (1991). "Structuring and Analyzing Values for Multiple-Issue Negotiations." In H. Peyton Young (ed.), *Negotiation Analysis.* Ann Arbor, MI: University of Michigan Press, pp. 131–151.

Kohler, David A., and R. Chandrasekaran (1971). "A Class of Sequential Games." *Operations Research* 19, no. 2 (March-April): 270–277.

Langreth, Robert, and Steven Lipin (1998). "Glaxo, SmithKline Reel in Battle of Egos." *Wall Street Journal,* February 25, p. A3.

Lavery, Norman G. (1996). "A New Arrow in the Mediator's Quiver: Adjusted Winner in the Context of Family Mediation." *ADR Forum: The Canadian Journal of Dispute Resolution* 10 (October): 4–5.

Lax, Jeffrey R. (1999). "Fair Division: A Format for the Debate on the Format of Debates." *PS: Political Science and Politics* 31, no. 1 (March).

Leng, Russell J., and William Epstein (1985). "Calculating Weapons Reductions." *Bulletin of the Atomic Scientists* 41, no. 2 (February): 39–41.

Levi, Primo (1979). *Moments of Reprieve: A Memoir of Auschwitz.* New York: Summit.

Lewis, Neil A. (1996a). "Panel on Debates Bars Perot, Calling Him Unelectable." *New York Times,* September 18, p. A1.

Lewis, Neil A. (1996b). "Clinton Aides Suggest Commission, Not Perot, May Have to Go." *New York Times,* September 20, p. A29.

Lewis, Neil A. (1996c). "Two Debates Set Between Dole and President." *New York Times,* September 22, p. 25.

Lipin, Steven (1996). "In Many Merger Deals, Ego and Pride Play Big Roles in Which Way Talks Go." *Wall Street Journal,* August 22, p. C1.

Lipin, Steven (1997). "The Market Bounceback: Merger Bankers Don't Bet on Increase in Leisure Time." *Wall Street Journal,* October 29, p. C16.

Lowry, S. Todd (1987). *The Archeology of Economic Ideas: The Classical Greek Tradition.* Durham, NC: Duke University Press.

Massoud, Tansa George (1998). "Fair Division, Adjusted Winner Procedure, and the Golan Heights." Preprint, Department of Political Science, Bucknell University.

Mitchell, Emily (1990). "Two for the Money." *Time* 135, no. 9 (February 26): 64.

Morris, Betsy (1998). "What's a Corporate Wife Worth?" *Fortune,*

February 2, pp. 65–78.

Morrow, David J. (1997). "The Card, at Least, Isn't Torn in Half." *New York Times*, December 7, p. BU11.

Moulin, Hervé (1995). *Cooperative Microeconomics: A Game-Theoretic Introduction*. Princeton, NJ: Princeton University Press.

"Move to Reopen Executive Divorce Case" (1997). *New York Times*, December 23, p. D8.

Nicolson, Nigel (ed.) (1992). *Vita and Harold: The Letters of Vita Sackville-West and Harold Nicolson*. New York: Putnam.

Plass, Paul (1995). *The Game of Death in Ancient Rome: Arena Sport and Political Suicide*. Madison, WI: University of Wisconsin Press.

Plass, Paul (1997). Private communication to Steven J. Brams (September 29).

Pocock, J. G. A. (ed.) (1977). *The Political Works of James Harrington*. Cambridge, UK: Cambridge University Press.

Pocock, J. G. A. (ed.) (1992). "Introduction." In James Harrington, *The Commonwealth of Oceana* and *A System of Politics*. Cambridge, UK: Cambridge University Press, pp. vii–xxvi.

Poundstone, William (1992). *Prisoner's Dilemma: John von Neumann, Game Theory, and the Puzzle of the Bomb*. New York: Doubleday.

Quandt, William B. (1986). *Camp David: Peacemaking and Politics*. Washington, DC: Brookings Institution.

Raiffa, Howard (1982). *The Art and Science of Negotiation*. Cambridge, MA: Harvard University Press.

Raiffa, Howard (1985). "Post-Settlement Settlements." *Negotiation Journal* 1, no. 1 (January): 9–12.

Raiffa, Howard (1993). "The Neutral Analyst: Helping Parties to Reach Better Solutions." In Lavinia Hall (ed.), *Negotiation: Strategies for Mutual Gain*. Newbury Park, CA: Sage, pp. 14–27.

Raiffa, Howard (1996). *Lectures on Negotiation Analysis*. Cambridge, MA: Program on Negotiation, Harvard Law School.

Raith, Matthias G. (1998a). "Supporting Cooperative Multi-Issue Negotiations." Preprint, Institute of Mathematical Economics, University of Bielefeld, Germany (June).

Raith, Matthias G. (1998b). "Fair-Negotiation Procedures." Preprint, Institute of Mathematical Economics, University of Bielefeld, Germany (July).

Raith, Matthias G., and Andreas Welzel (1998). "Adjusted Winner: An Algorithm for Implementing Bargaining Solutions in Multi-Issue Negotiations." Preprint, Institute of Mathematical Economics,

University of Bielefeld, Germany (March).

Reijnierse, J. H., and J. A. M. Potters (1998). "On Finding an Envy-Free Pareto Optimal-Division." *Mathematical Programming* 83, no. 2 (October): 291–311.

Rhoads, Christopher, *et al.* (1998). "Swiss Banks' $25 Billion Merger Sparks Friction, Lofty Defections." *Wall Street Journal*, April 3, p. A15.

Riker, William H. (1986). *The Art of Political Manipulation*. New Haven, CT: Yale University Press.

Riker, William H. (1996). *The Strategy of Rhetoric: Campaigning for the American Constitution*. New Haven, CT: Yale University Press.

Robertson, Jack, and William Webb (1998). *Cake-Cutting Algorithms: Be Fair If You Can*. Natick, MA: A K Peters.

Ryback, Timothy W. (1998). "The Man Who Swallowed Chrysler." *New Yorker*, November 16, pp. 80–89.

Saaty, Thomas L. (1995). *The Fundamentals of Decision Making and Priority with the Analytic Hierarchy Process*. Pittsburgh, PA: RWS Publications.

Saaty, Thomas L., and Luis G. Vargas (1991). *Predictions, Projection, and Forecasting: Applications of the Analytic Hierarchy Process in Economics, Finance, Politics, Games, and Sports*. Boston: Kluwer Academic.

Salter, Stephen H. (1986). "Stopping the Arms Race." *Issues in Science and Technology* 2, no. 2 (Winter): 74–92.

Sebenius, James K. (1984). *Negotiating the Law of the Sea*. Cambridge, MA: Harvard University Press.

Sebenius, James K. (1992). "Negotiation Analysis: A Characterization and Review." *Management Science* 38, no. 1 (January): 18–38.

Sharp, Tony (1975). *The Wartime Alliance and the Zonal Division of Germany*. Oxford, UK: Clarendon Press.

Simon, Herbert A. (1991). *Models of My Life*. New York: Basic.

Sims, Gideon Y. (1996). "Adjusted Winner Applied to the 1996 Presidential Debates." Unpublished term paper written for Steven J. Brams, New York University.

Singer, Mark (1997). "Trump Solo." *New Yorker*, May 19, pp. 57–70.

Smith, Jean Edward (1963). *The Defense of Berlin*. Baltimore: Johns Hopkins University Press.

Stein, Janice Gross (1993). "The Political Economy of Security Agreements: The Linked Costs of Failure at Camp David." In Peter B. Evans, Harold Jacobson, and Robert Putnam (eds.), *Double-Edged Diplomacy: International Bargaining and Domestic Politics*. Berkeley, CA: University of California Press, pp. 77–103.

Taylor, Alan D. (1995). *Mathematics and Politics: Strategy, Voting, Power and Proof.* New York: Springer-Verlag.

Taylor, Alan D. (1998). "Taking Turns." Preprint, Department of Mathematics, Union College, New York.

Telhami, Shibley (1990). *Power and Leadership in International Bargaining: The Path to the Camp David Accords.* New York: Columbia University Press.

Thomas, Elizabeth Marshall (1959). *The Harmless People.* New York: Alfred A. Knopf (2d ed., Vintage, 1989).

Trump, Donald (1987). *Trump: The Art of the Deal.* New York: Random House.

Trump, Donald (1990). *Trump: Surviving at the Top.* New York: Random House.

Trump, Donald (1997). *Trump: The Art of the Comeback.* New York: Random House.

Weber, Bruce (1997). "Donald and Marla Are Headed for Divestiture." *New York Times,* May 3, p. 27.

Whitney, Craig R. (1998). "Beyond the Grave, DNA Haunts Yves Montand," *New York Times,* March 12, p. A4.

Willson, Stephen J. (1998). "Fair Division Using Linear Programming." Preprint, Department of Mathematics, Iowa State University.

Wilson, James Q. (1993). *The Moral Sense.* New York: Free Press.

Young, H. Peyton (ed.) (1991). *Negotiation Analysis.* Ann Arbor, MI: University of Michigan Press.

Young, H. Peyton (1994). *Equity in Theory and Practice.* Princeton, NJ: Princeton University Press.

Young, H. Peyton (1995). "Dividing the Indivisible." *American Behavioral Scientist* 38, no. 6 (May): 904–920.

"Yves Montand DNA Says No Paternity" (1998). *New York Times,* June 12, p. A3.

INDEX